LYNNE PICKERING

ART

& INTERIORS 2

Nudes & Beach Art

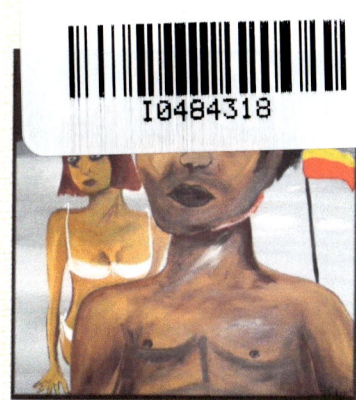

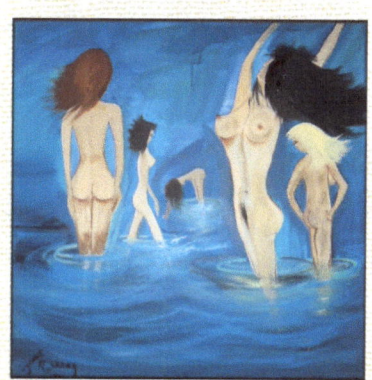

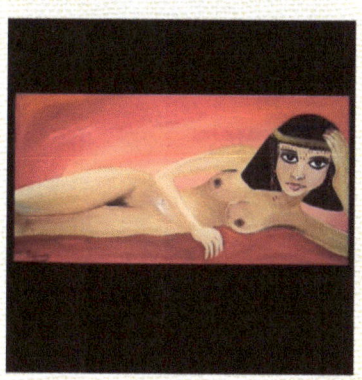

Original art by Lynne Pickering

Over 5,500 paintings sold to over 30 countries world wide.

UK, USA, Mexico, France, Spain,Singapore, China, Japan, Germany, Switzerland , New Zealand, South Africa, Australia, Papua New Guinea, Figi, Canada,Russia,Portugal,Switzerland,Scotland, Ireland, Brazil, Argentina, Granada, Caribbean, United Emirates, Isle of Man, Jersey, Il'd de France,Iceland,Luxembourg, Hawaii. Art galleries in Hollywood, to castles in UK. Portraits that have been on tour of Australia for 8 months at a time in 2007 & 2008 with the Bald Archy finalist. Lynne gets inspiration for Nature , the ocean, wildlife and people. Her nudes are popular in New York and worldwide. She also writes adult novels and illustrates children' s books. Enjoy this book of her art.

INDEX

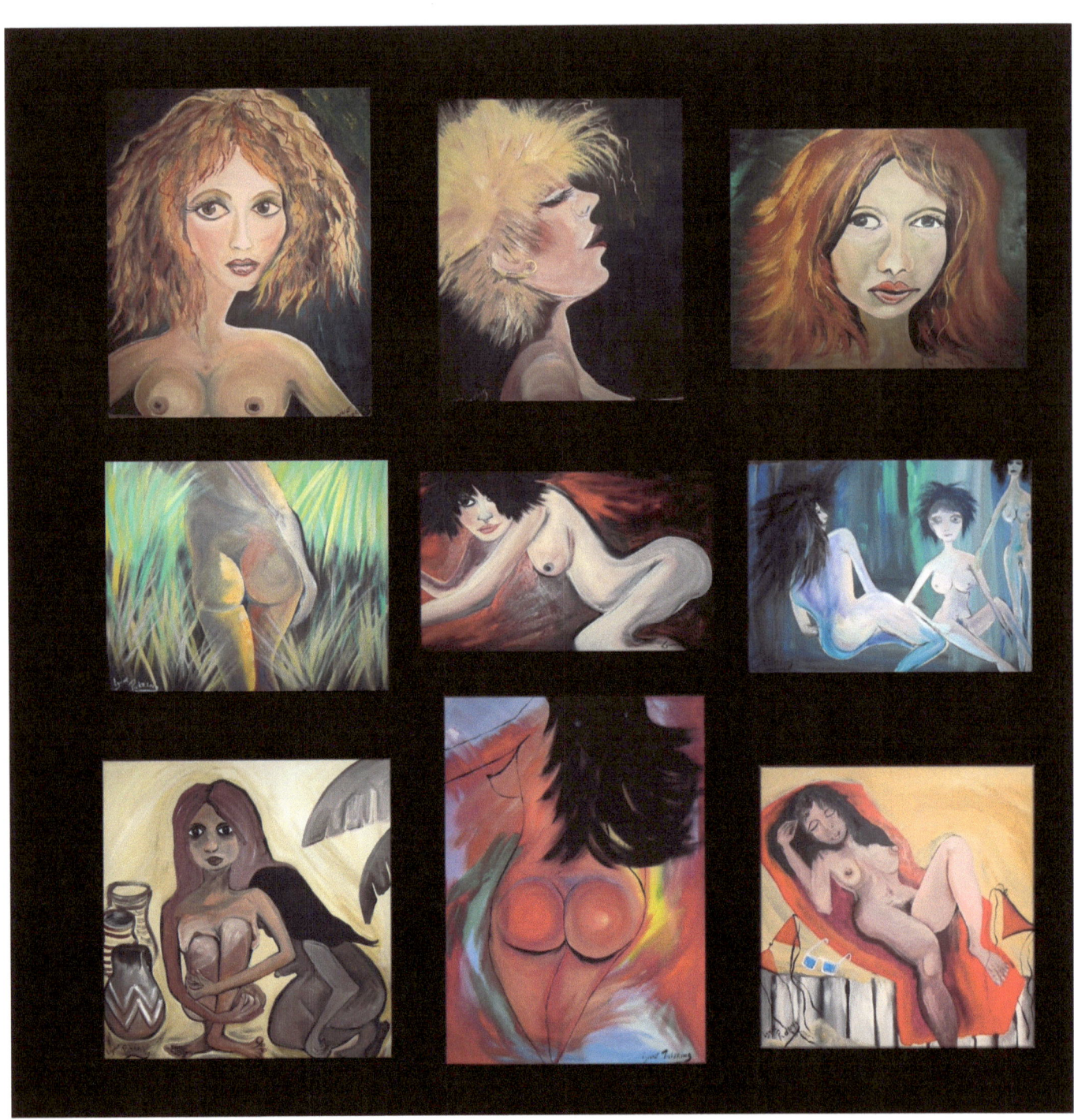

Large acrylic 4ft x3ft reclining nude

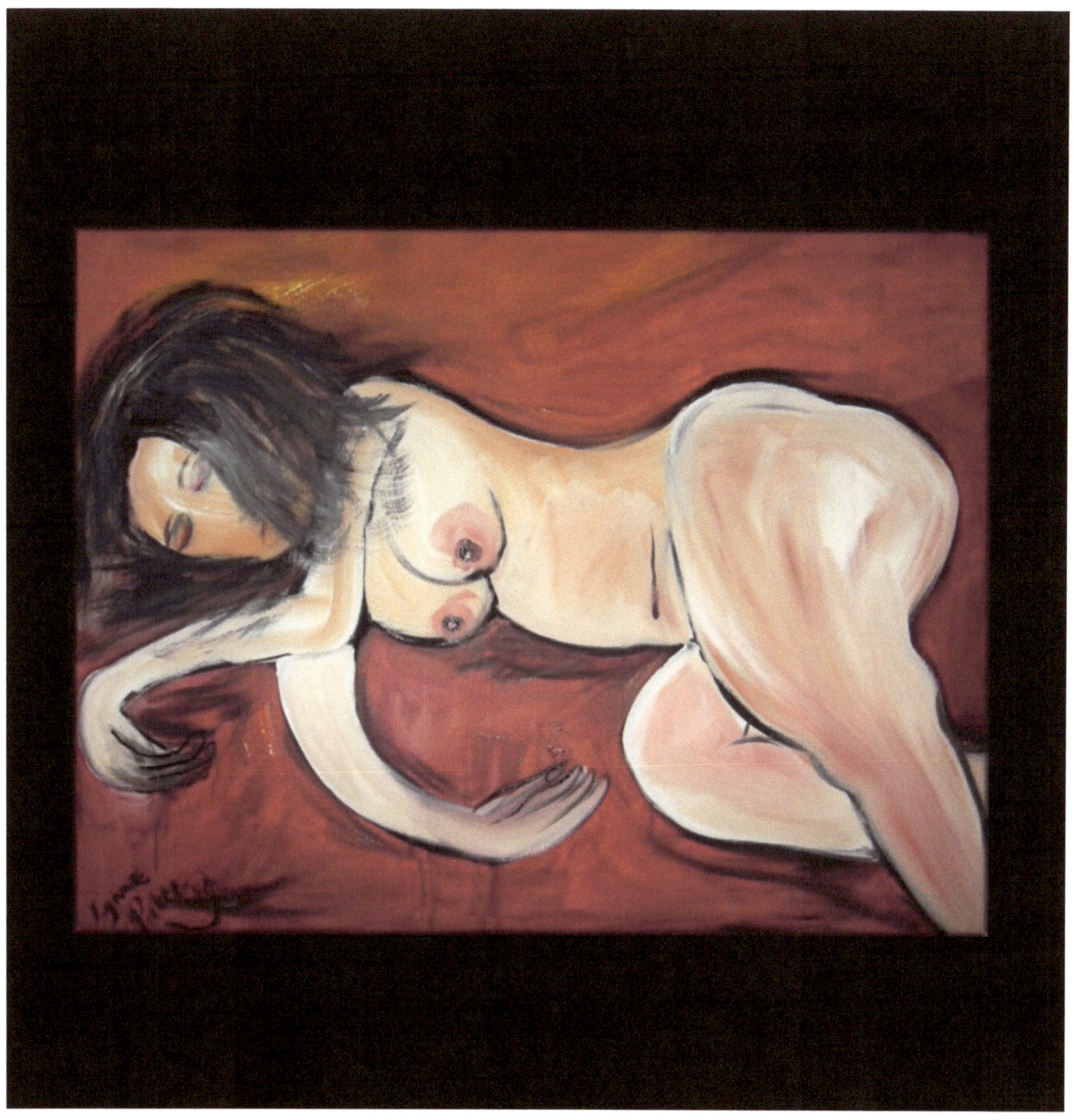

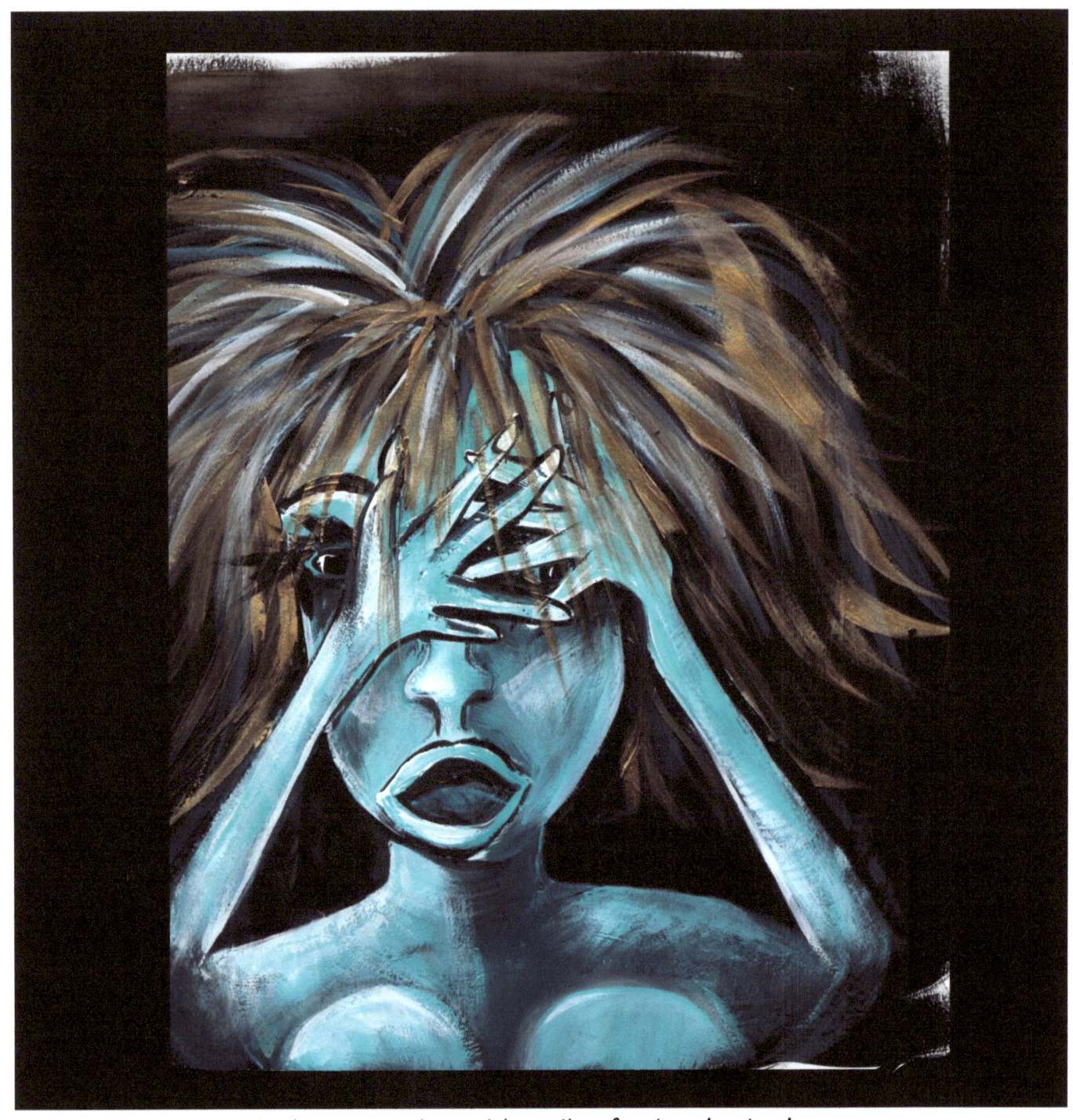

Watercolor " Shocked." For Author Chloe Silva for her book about Maya.

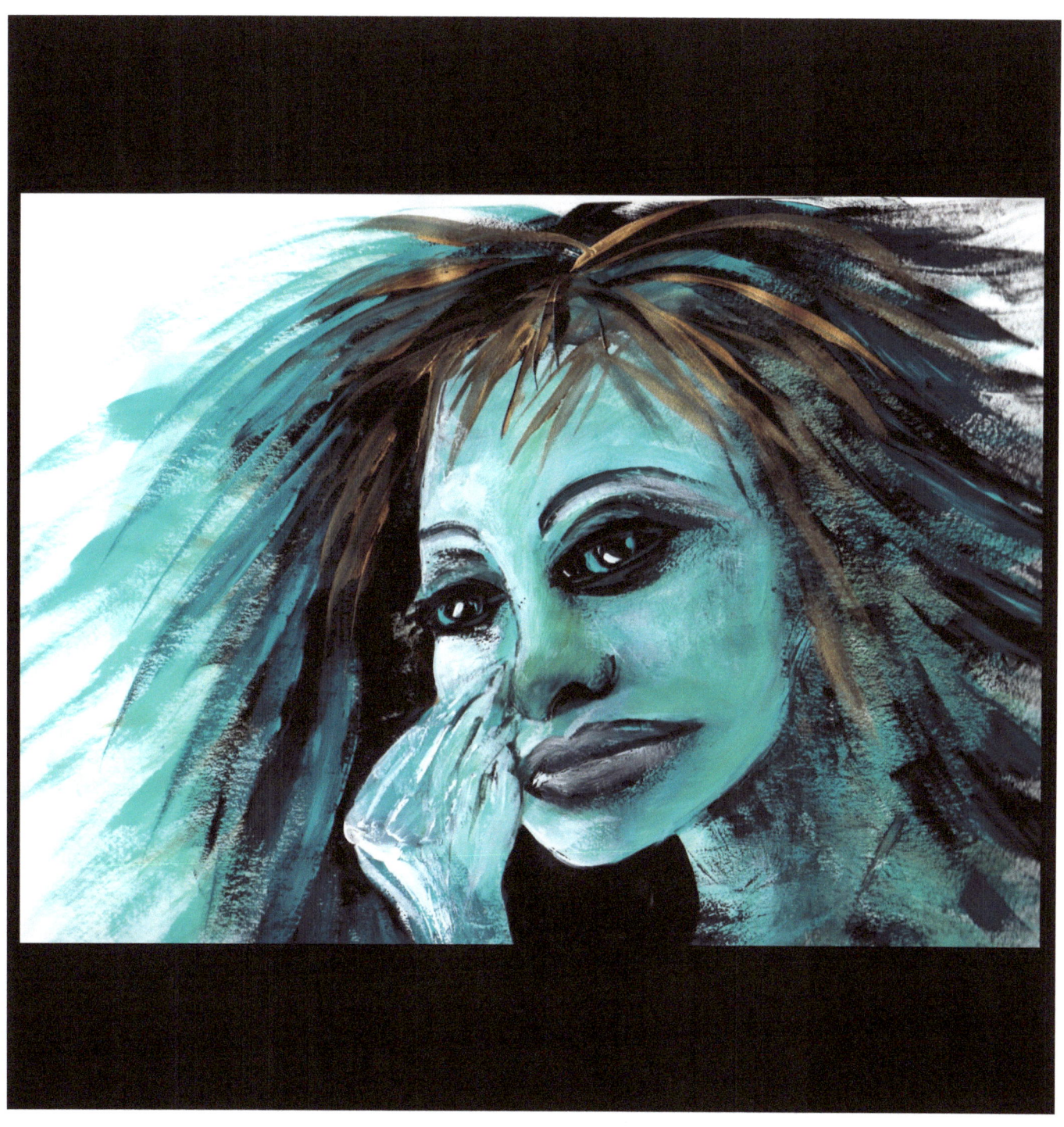

Watercolor on textured art paper

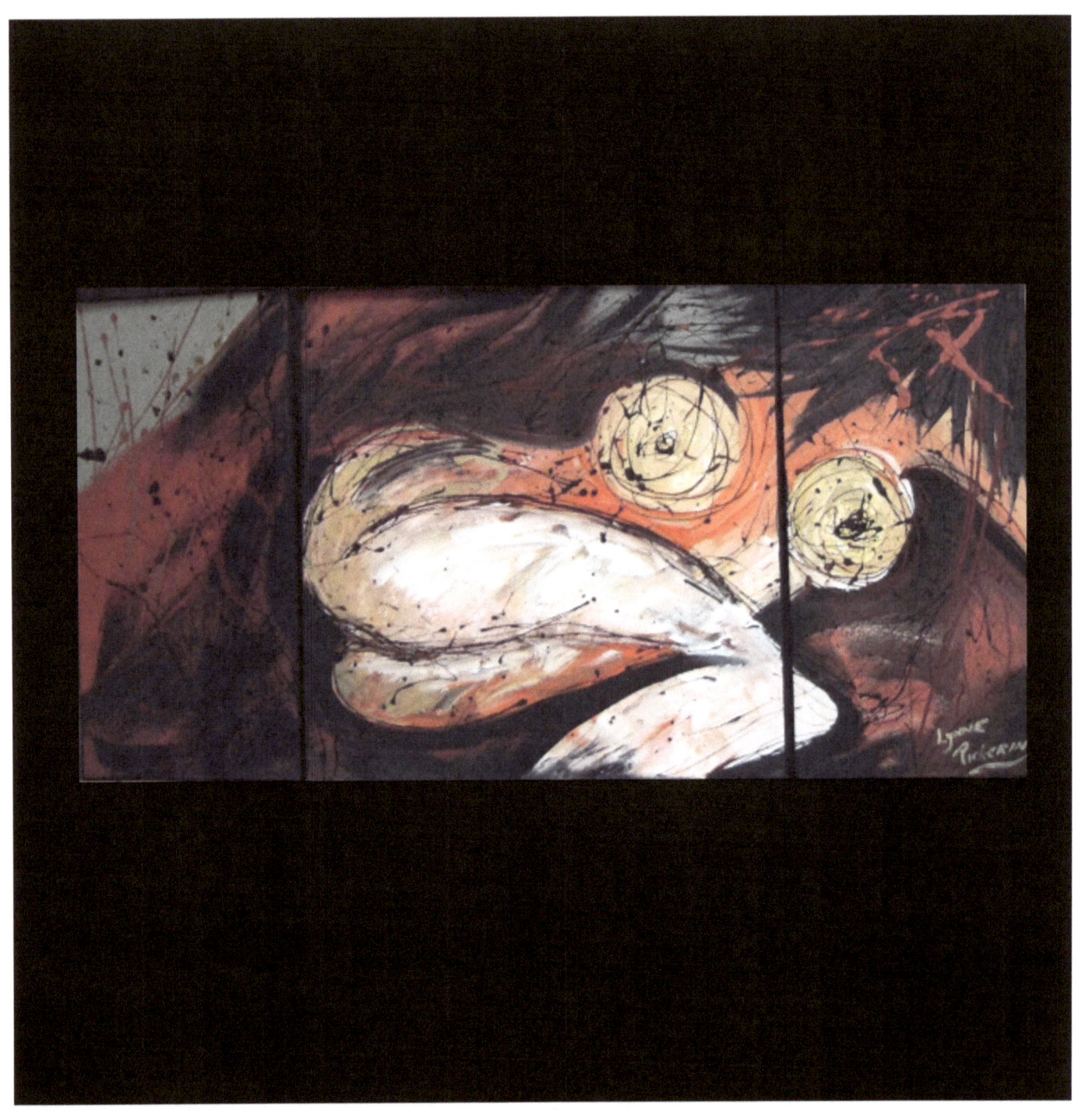

Abstract nude 4feet 2ft. Acrylic on canvas

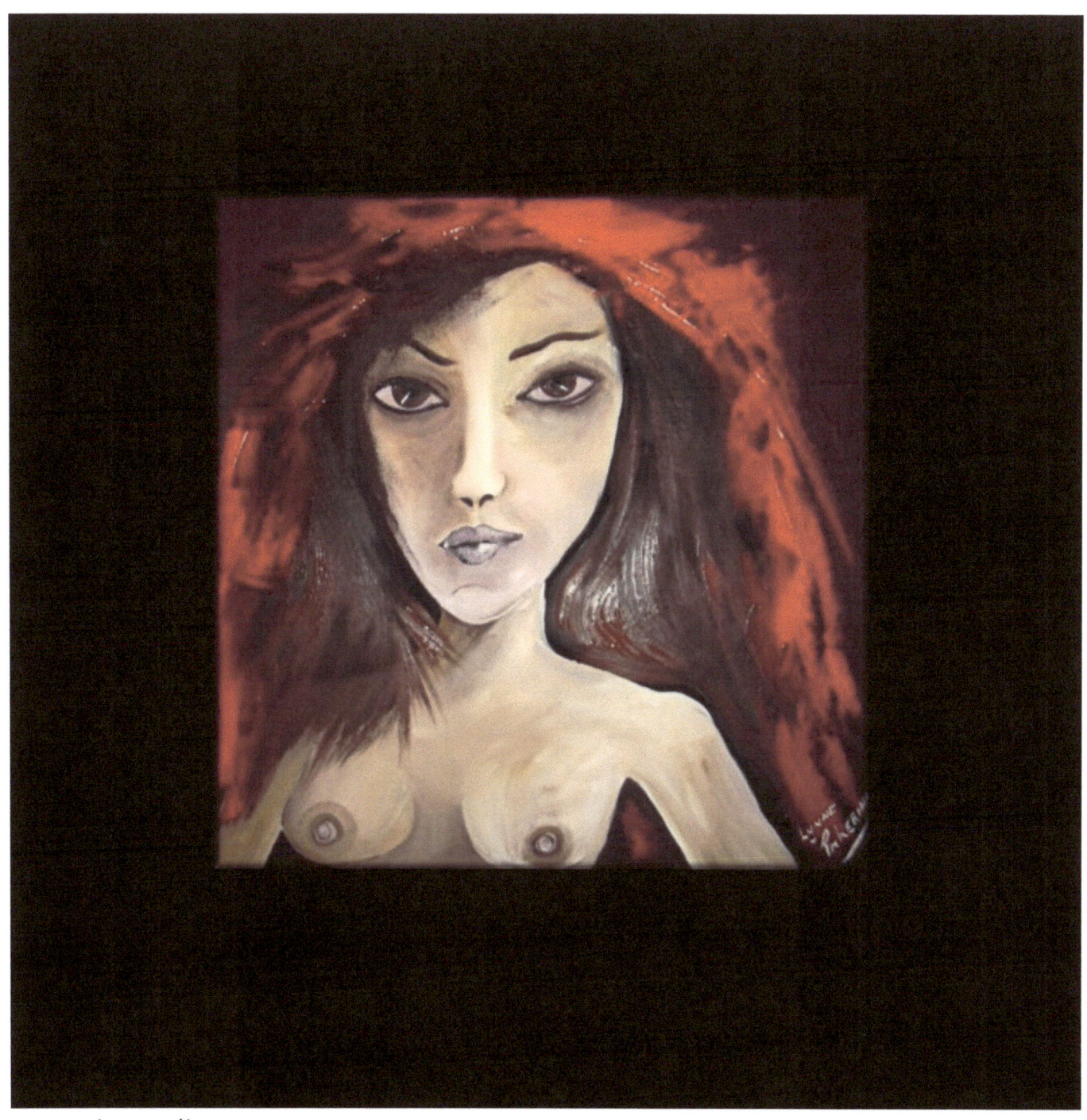

Portrait acrylic 24x24" on canvas

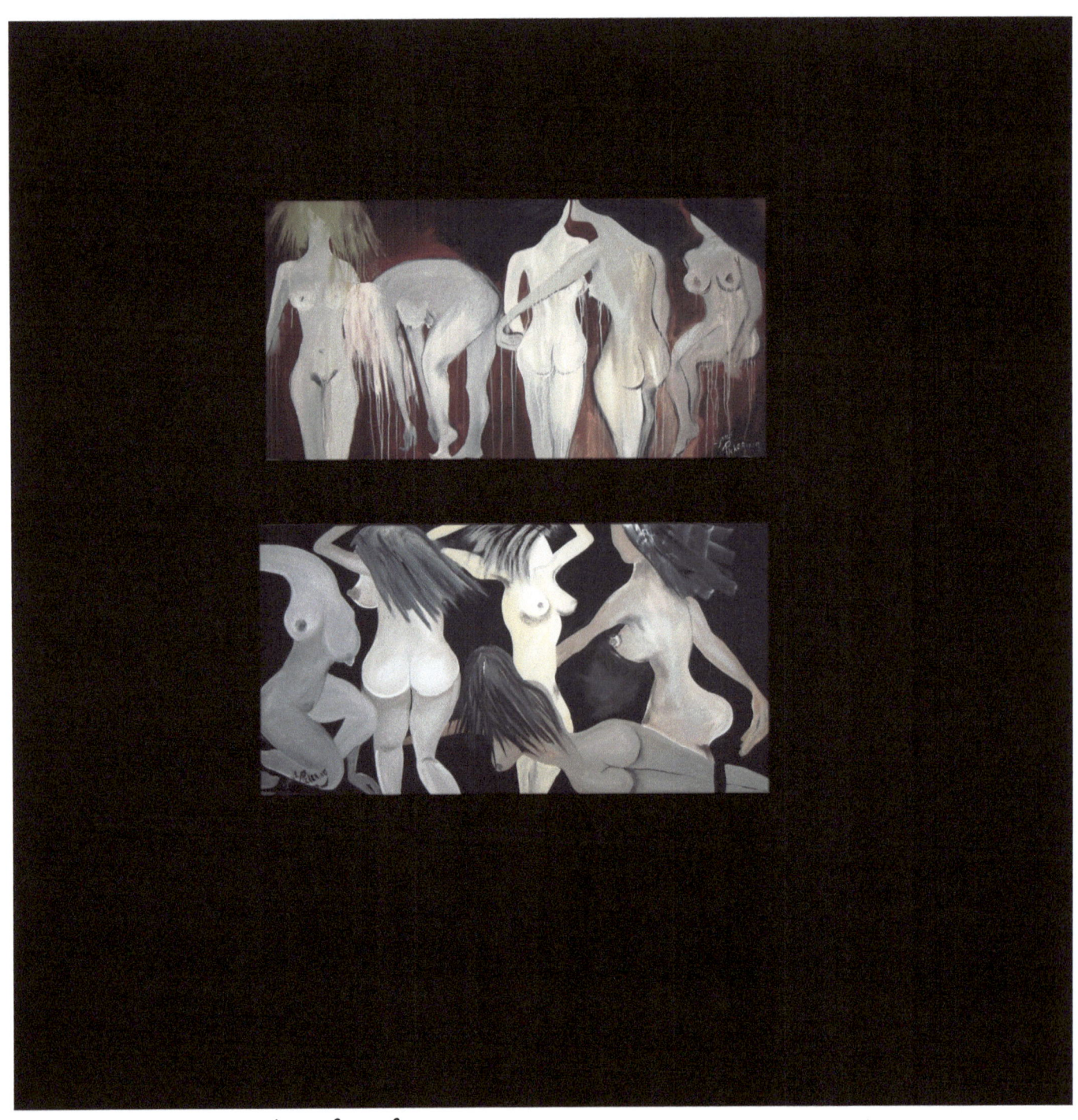

WALL MURALS Nudes 6ft x3ft

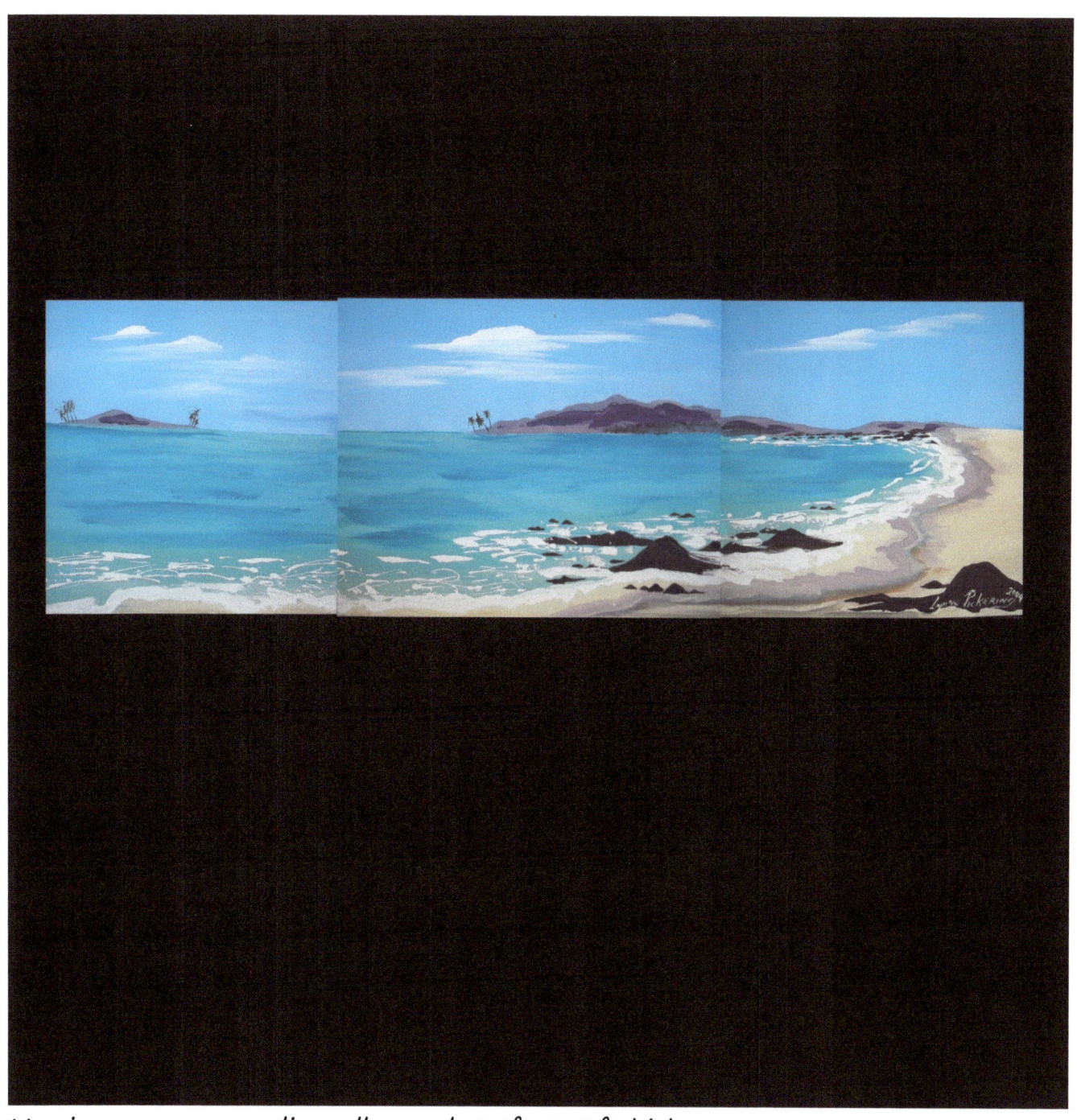

Massive seascape acrylic wall mural 10feet x3ft high

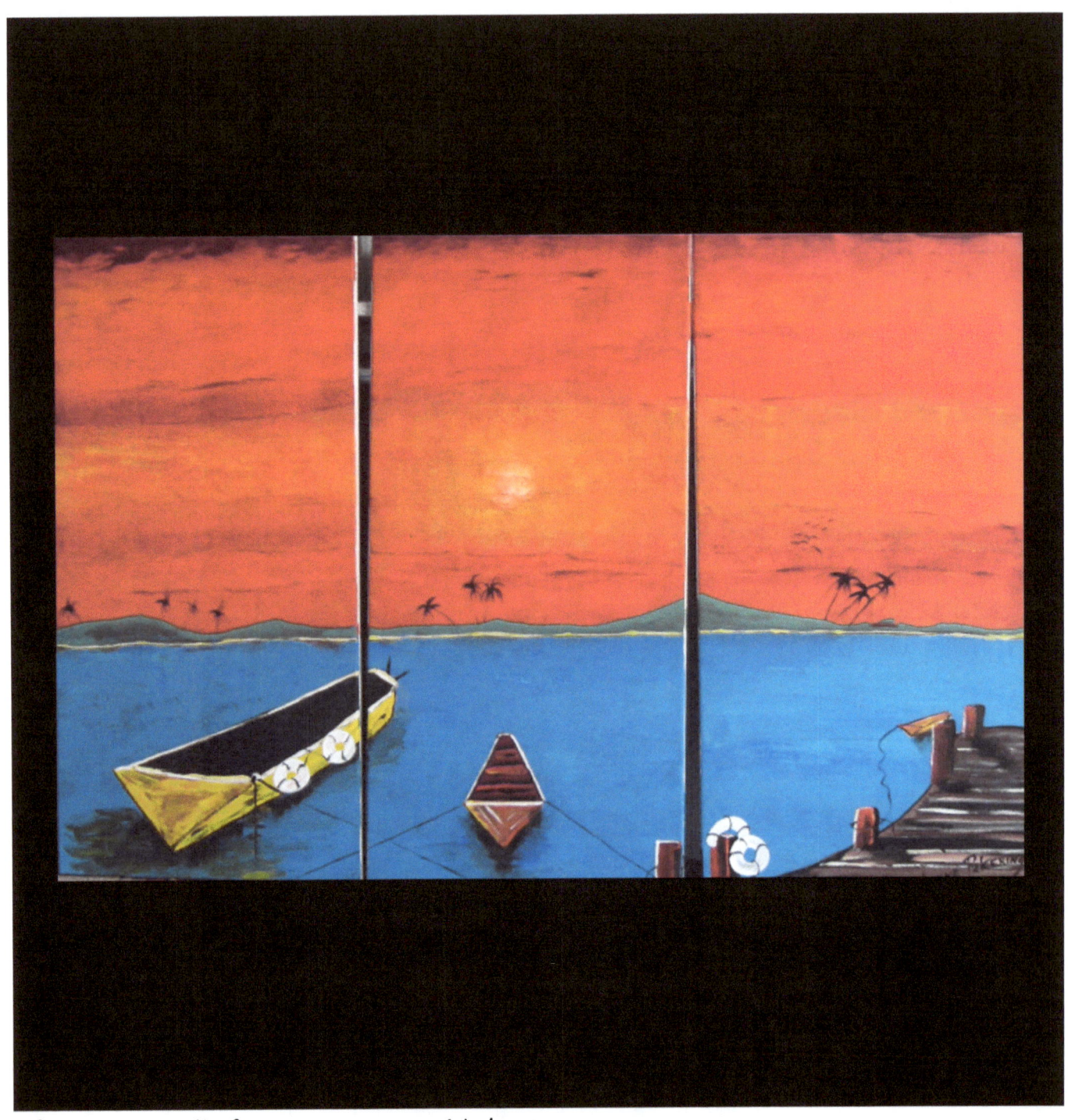

4ft x32" acrylic fauve seascape with boats

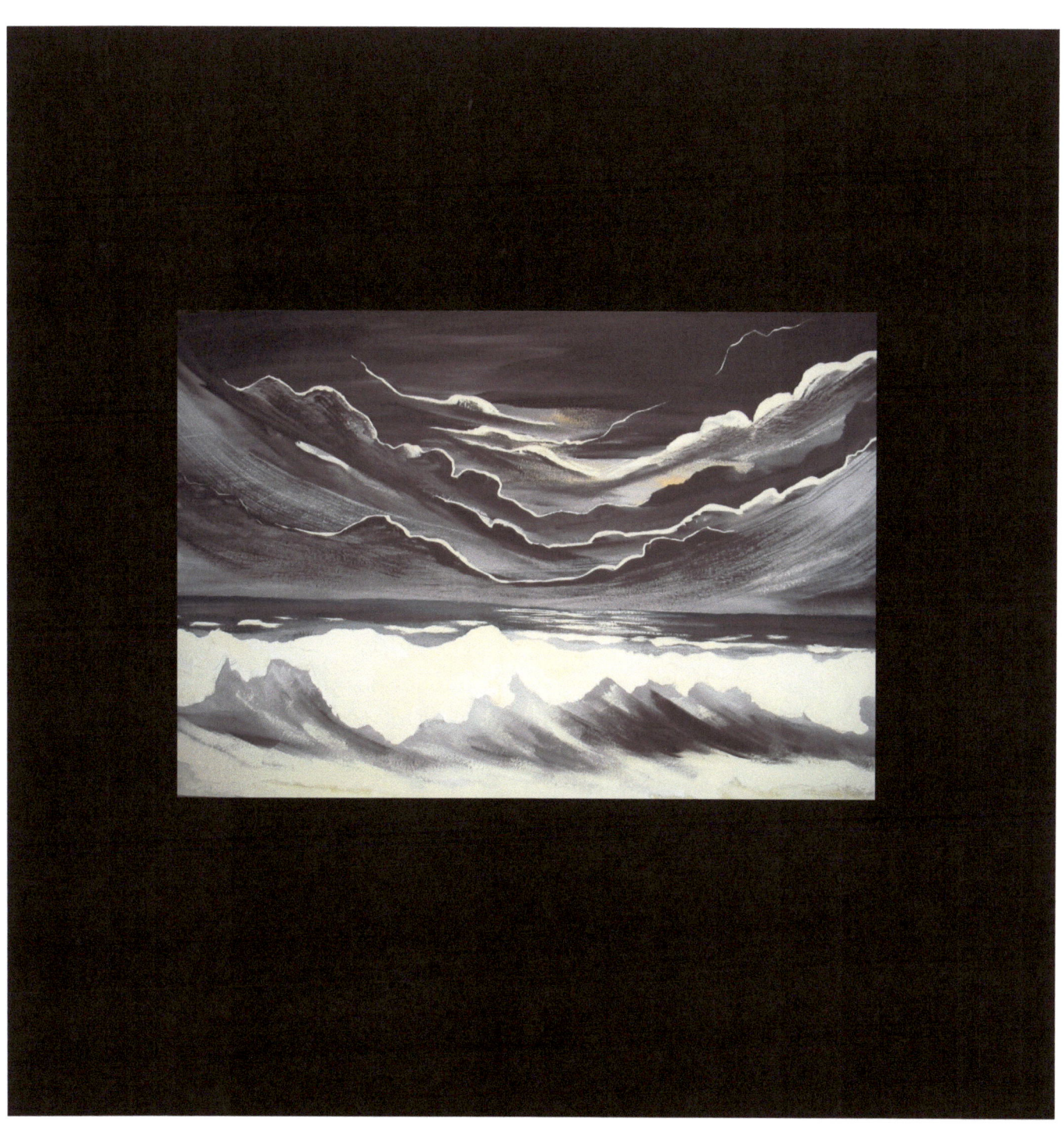

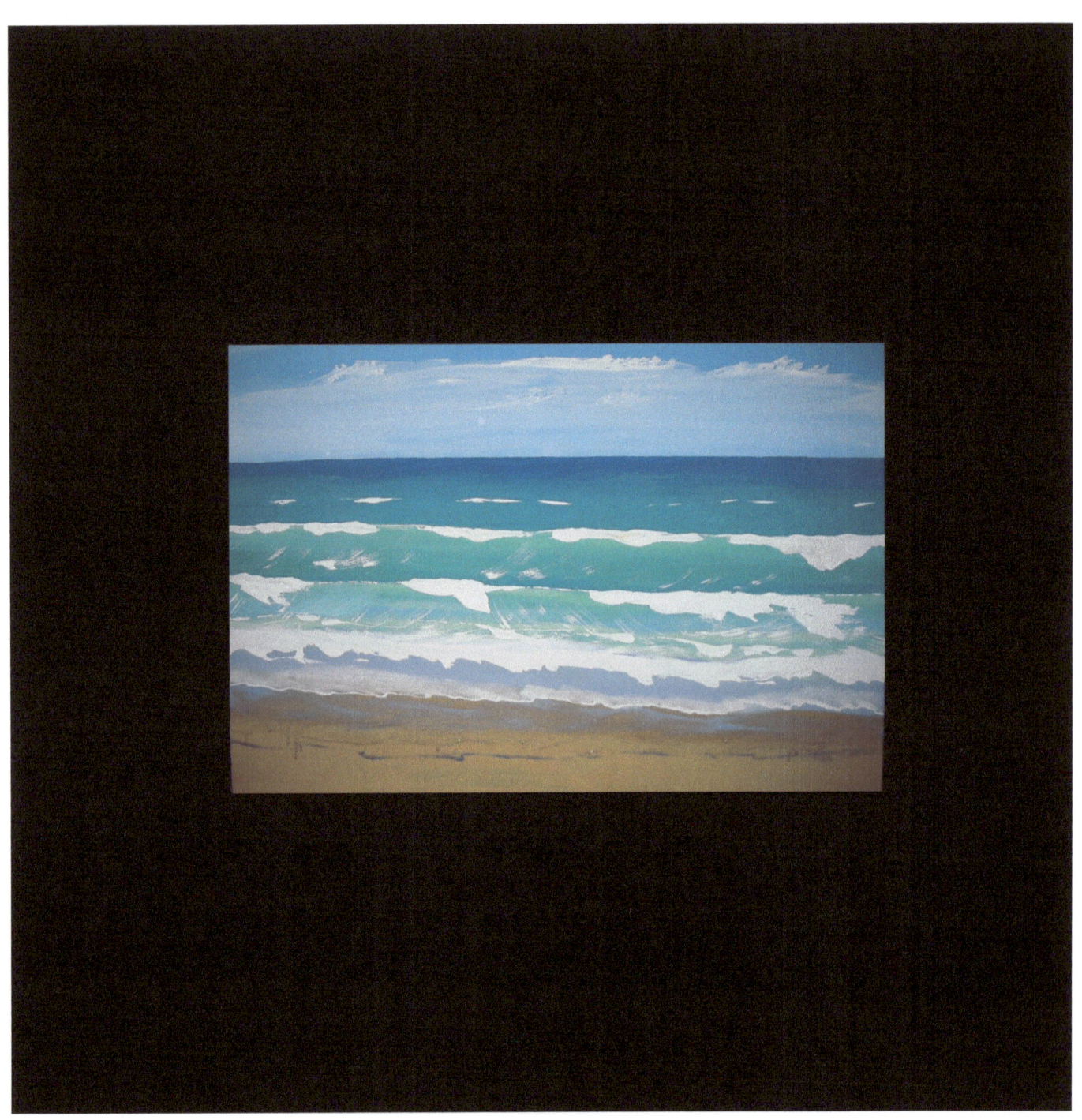

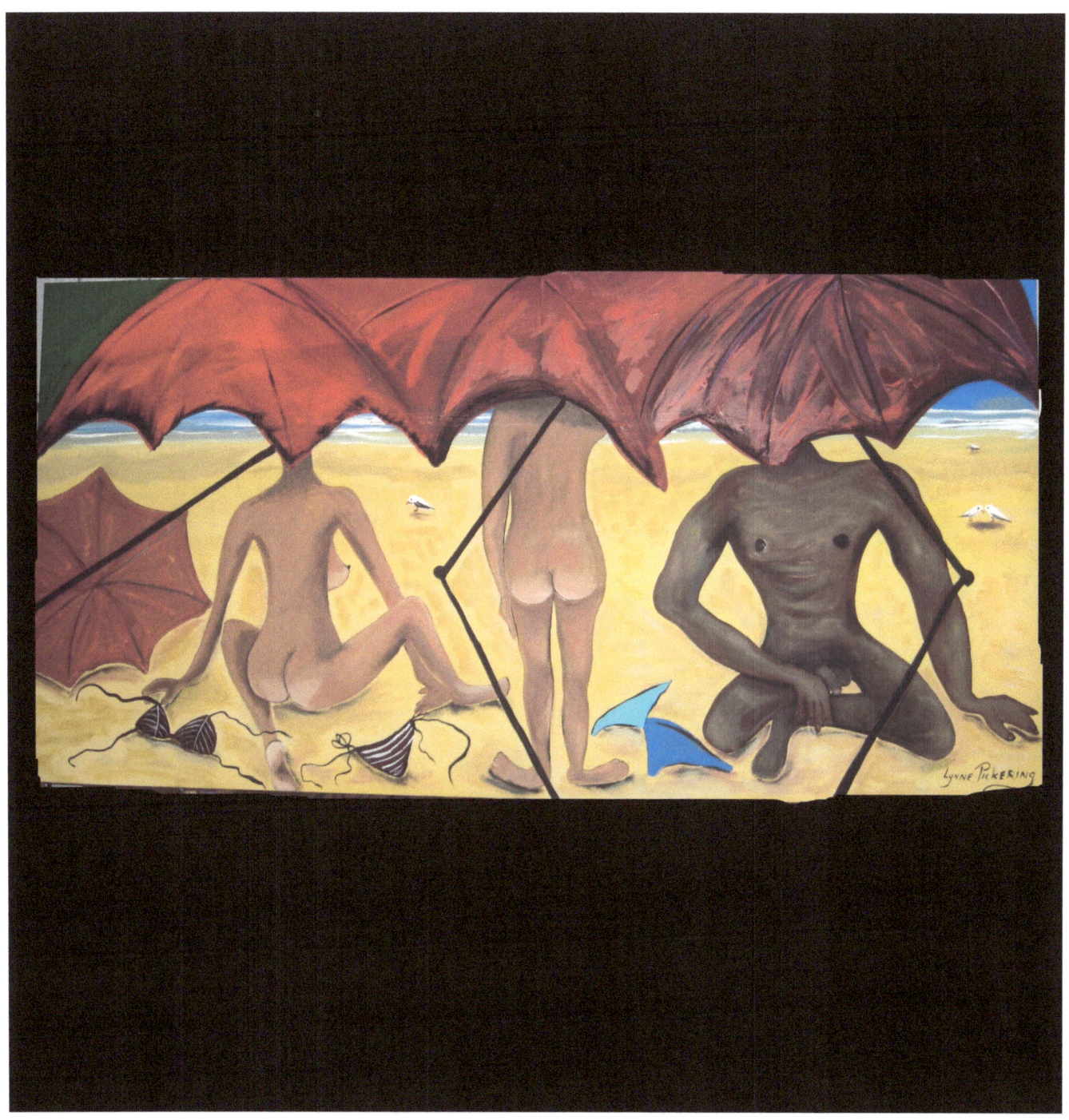

Nude Beach for Restaurant Cafe in Sydney Australia 6ft x3ft.

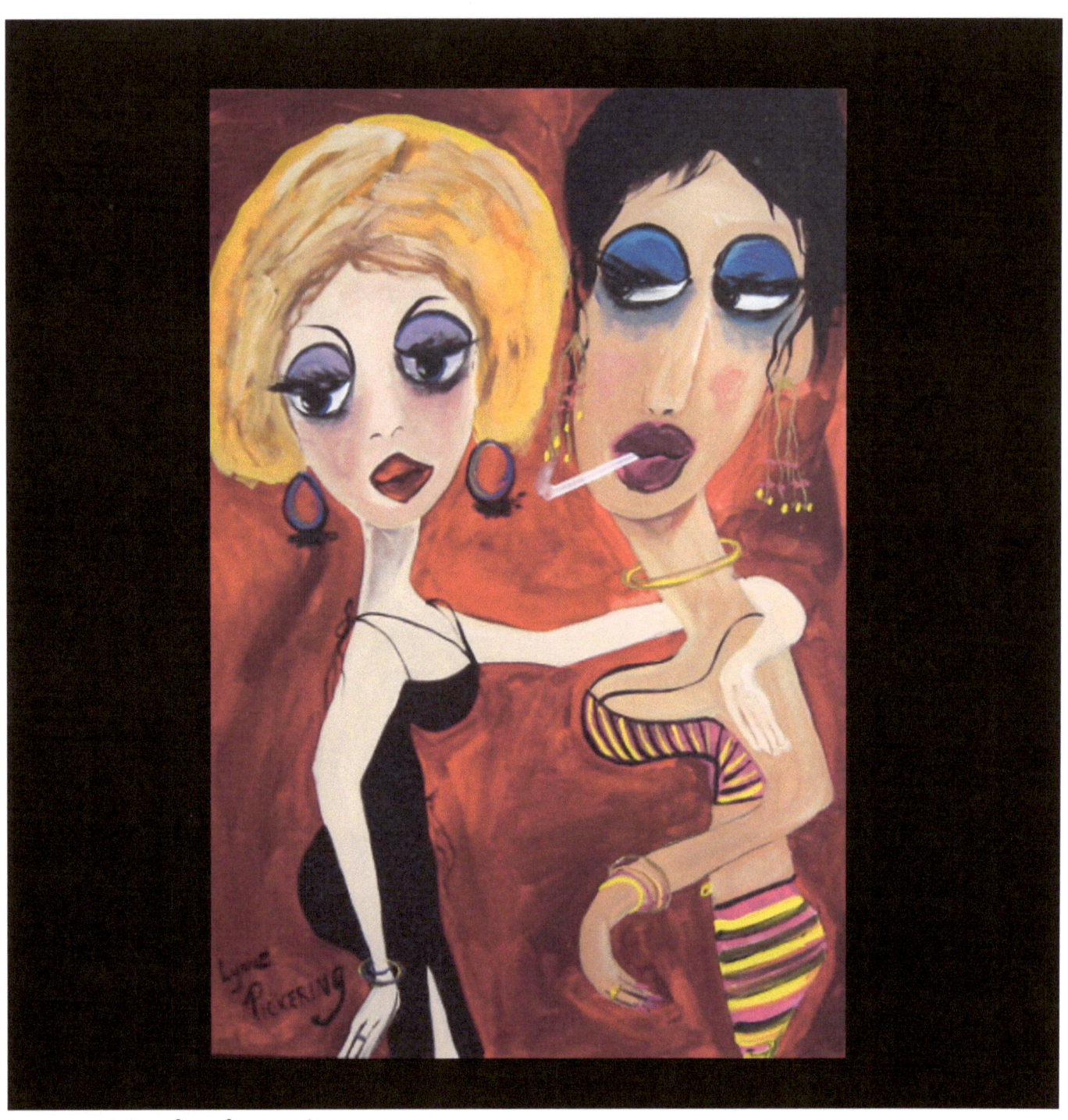

Party Girls 3ftx2ft acrylic

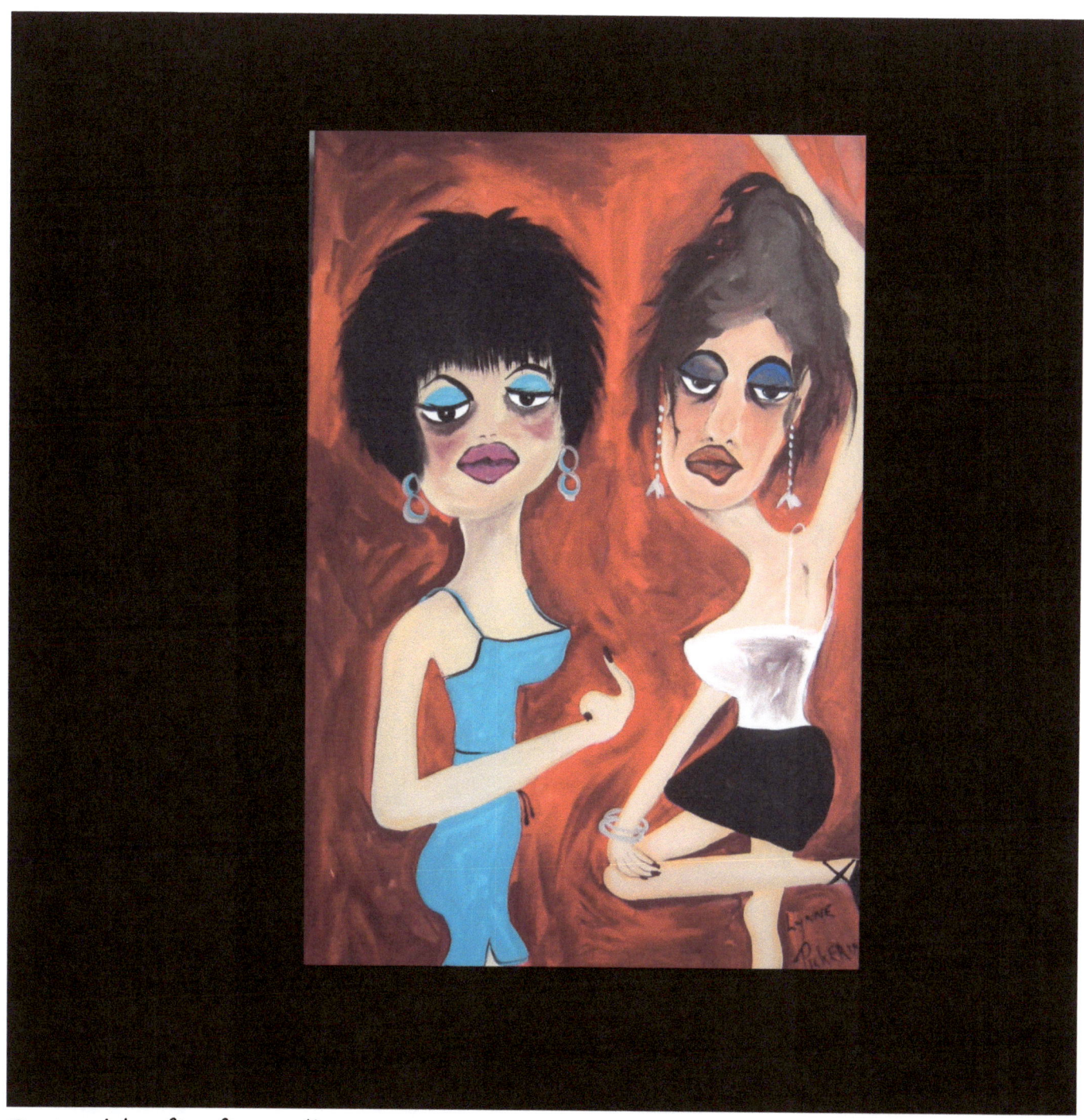

Party girls 3ftx2ft acrylic

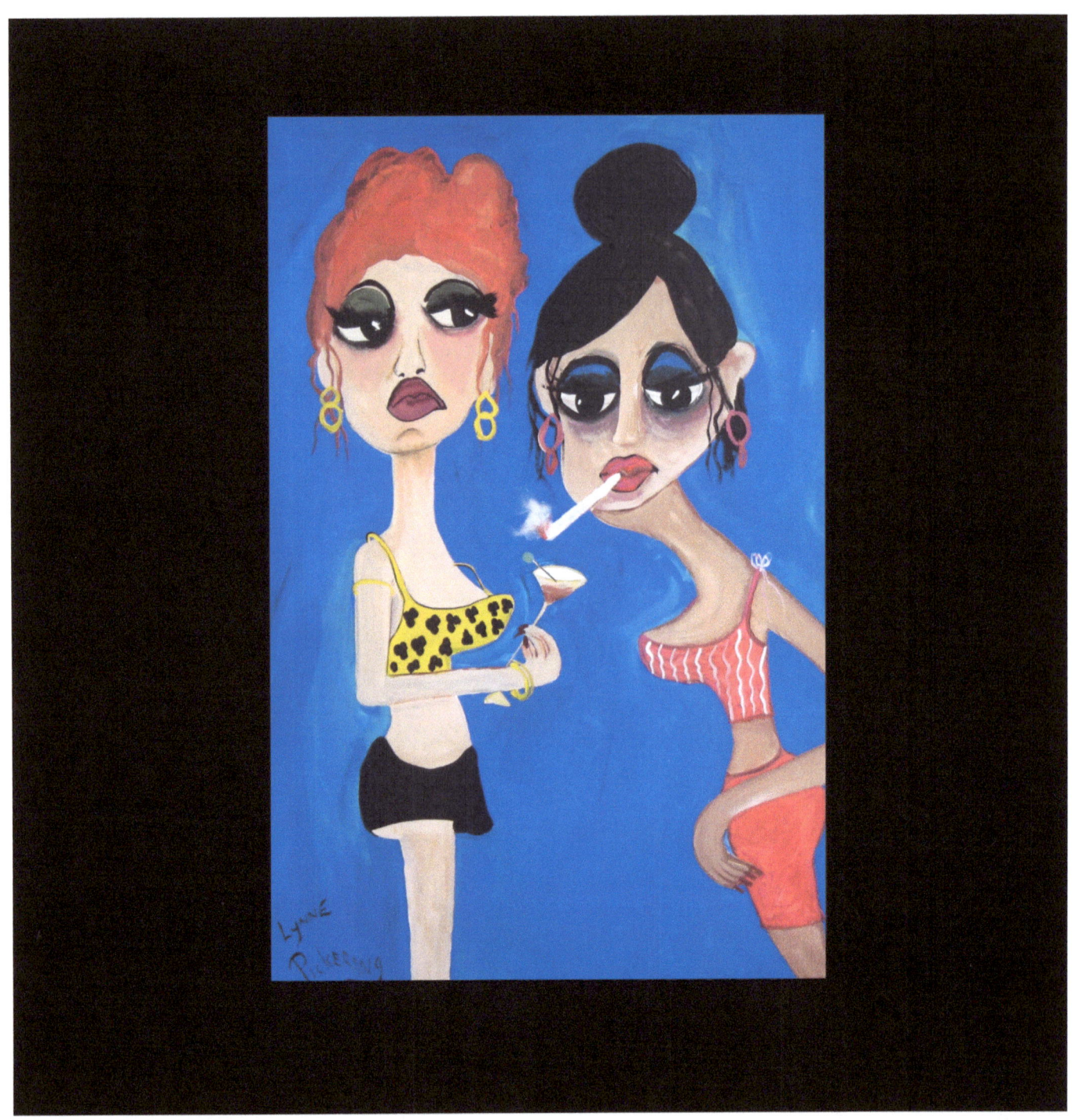

Beach party girls 3ftx2ft acrylic

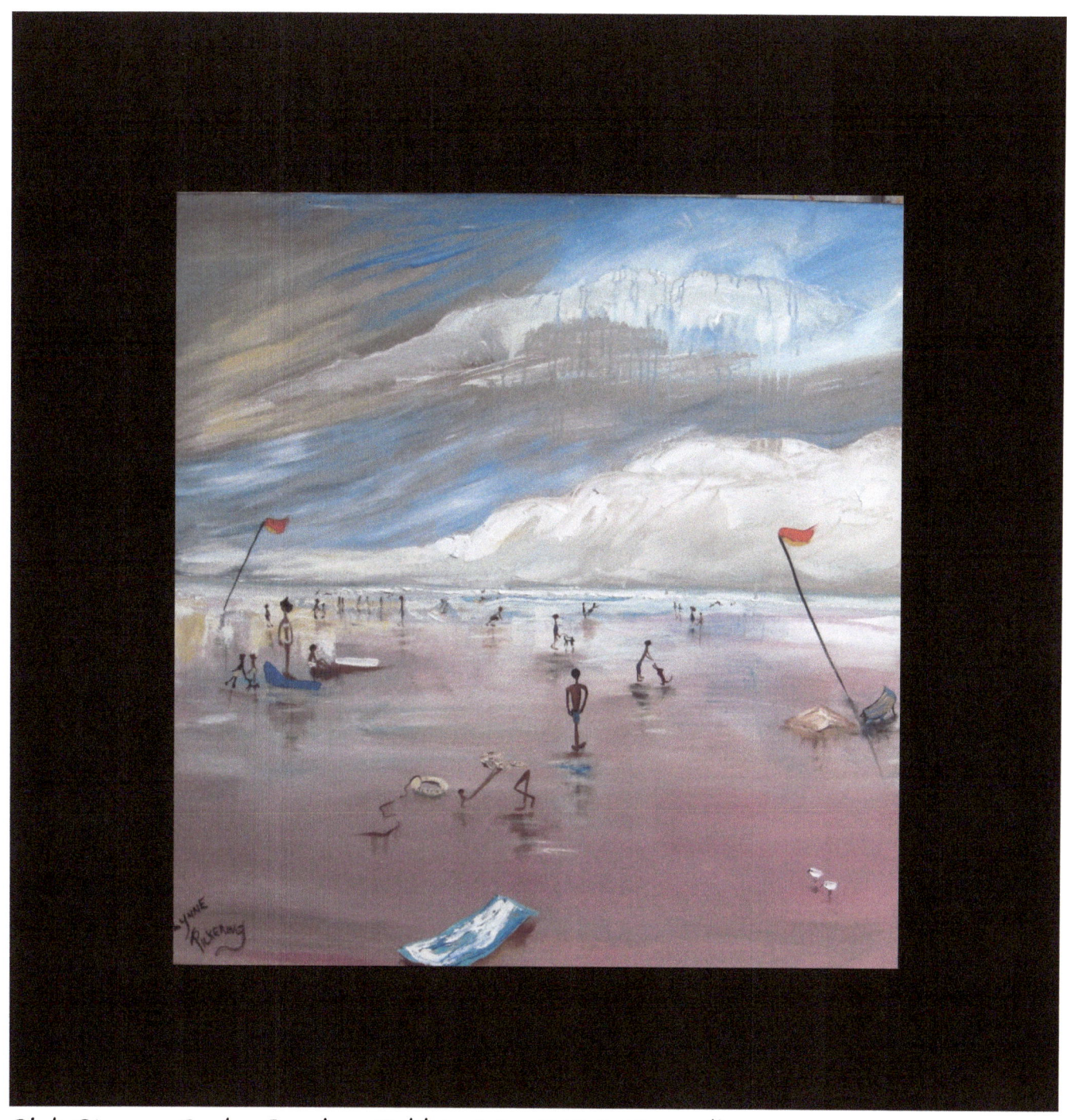

Pink Stormy Funky Beach   Sold to LA   36"x36" acrylic

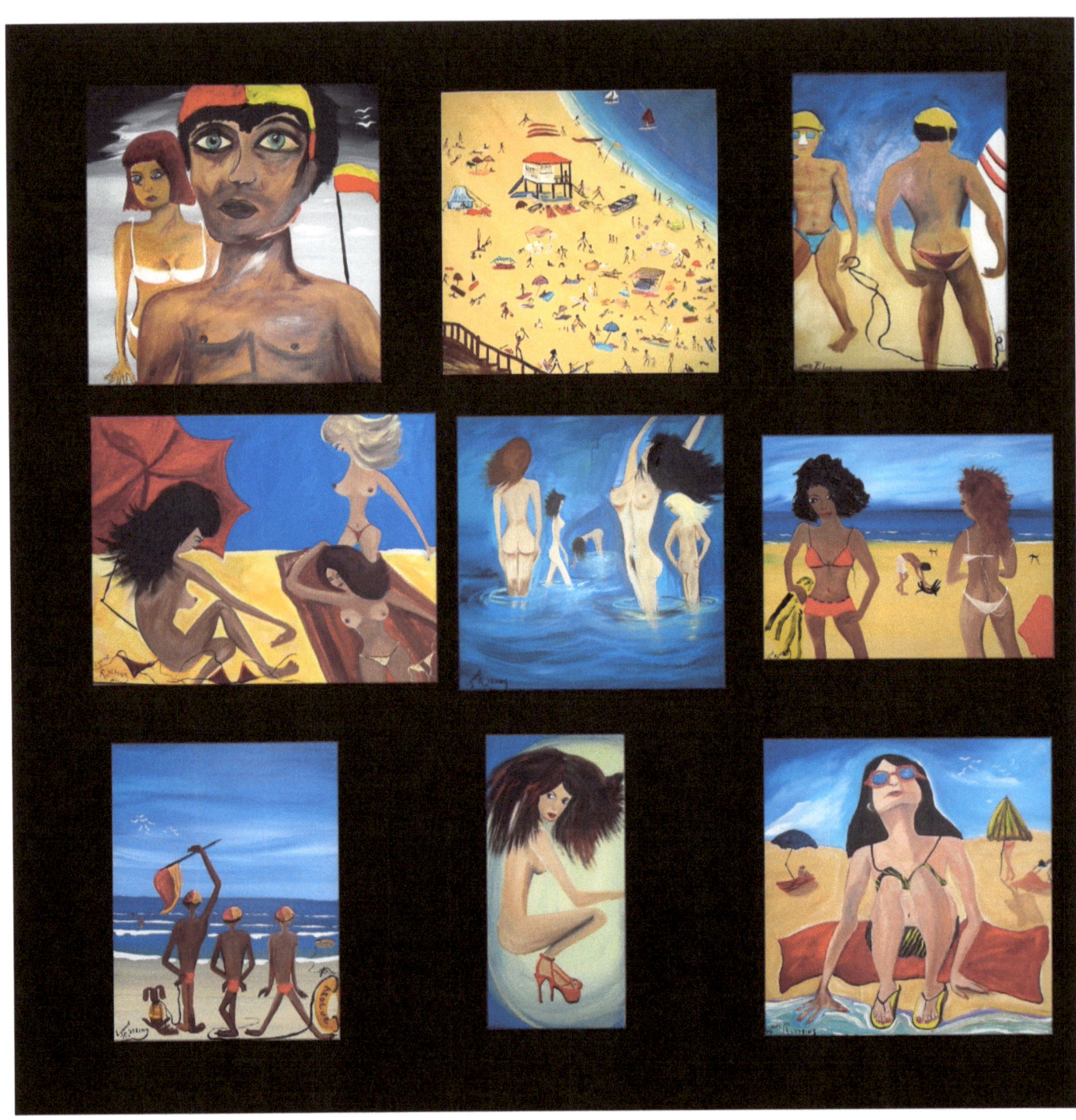

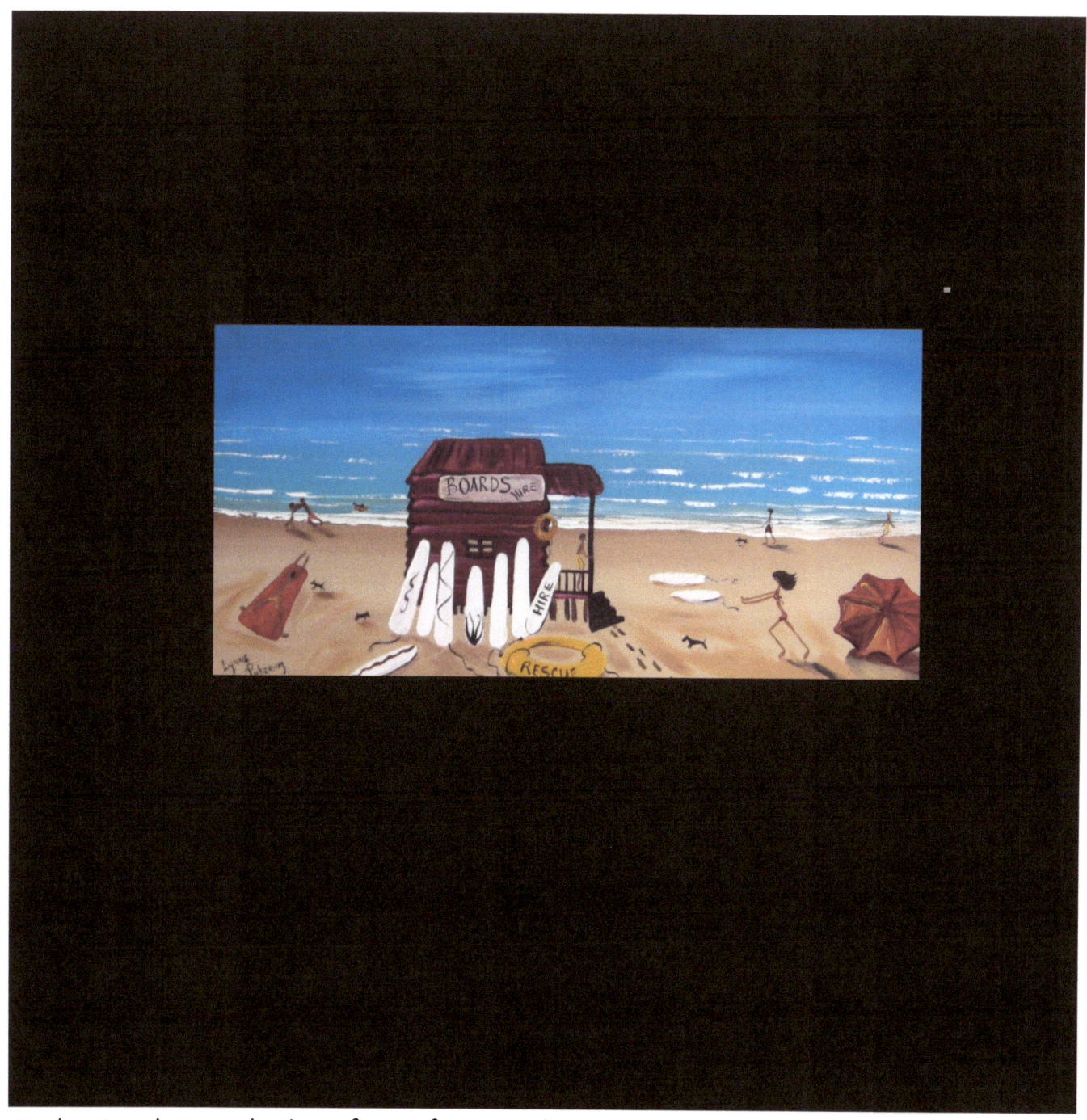

Funky Beach Board Hire 4feetx2feet acrylic

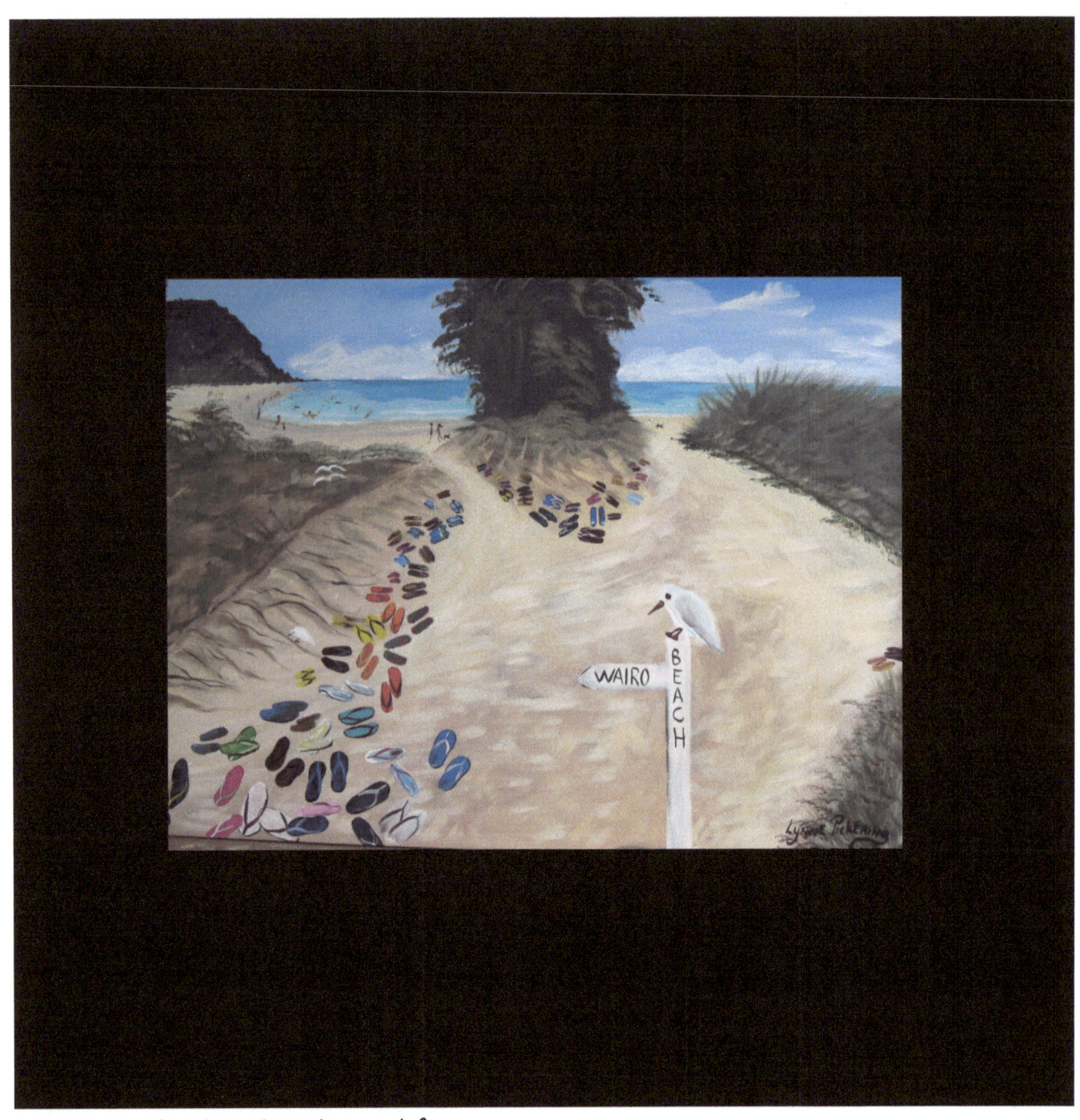

Wairo Beach Victoria Thongs left

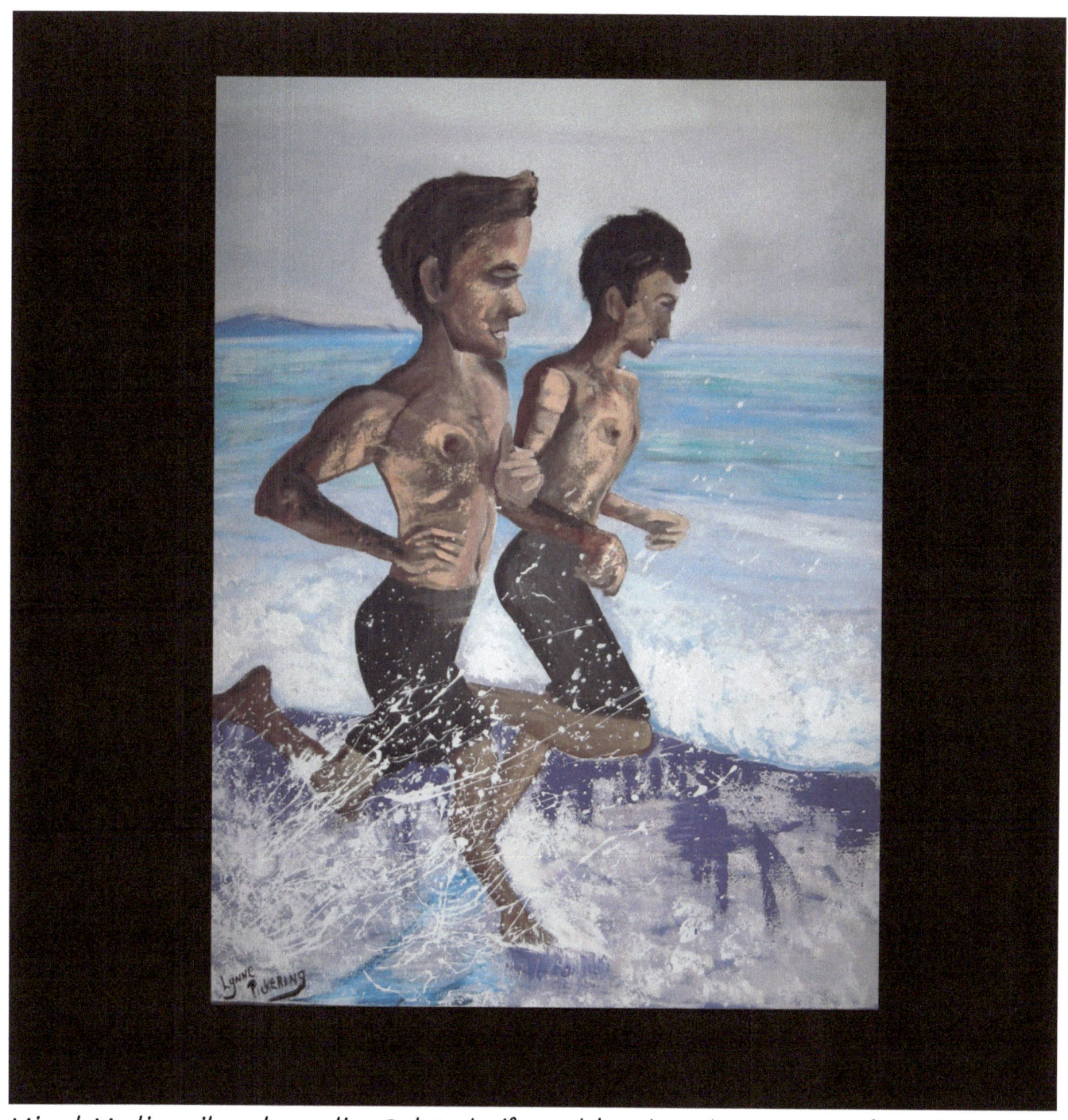

Mixed Media oil and acrylic Palate knife and brush   The Joggers (for sale)

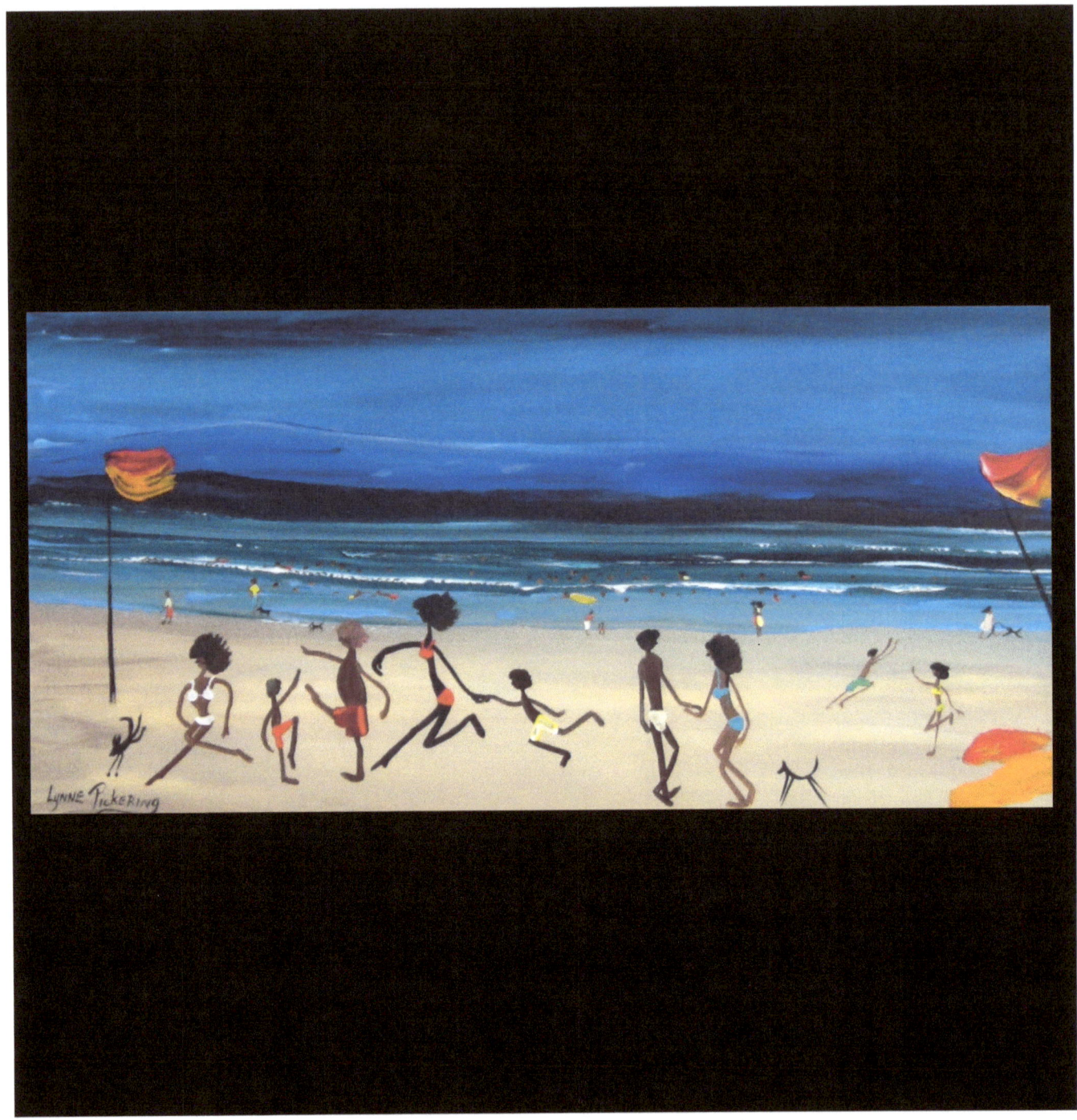

Funky Beach   Congo Line 4ft x2ft acrylic

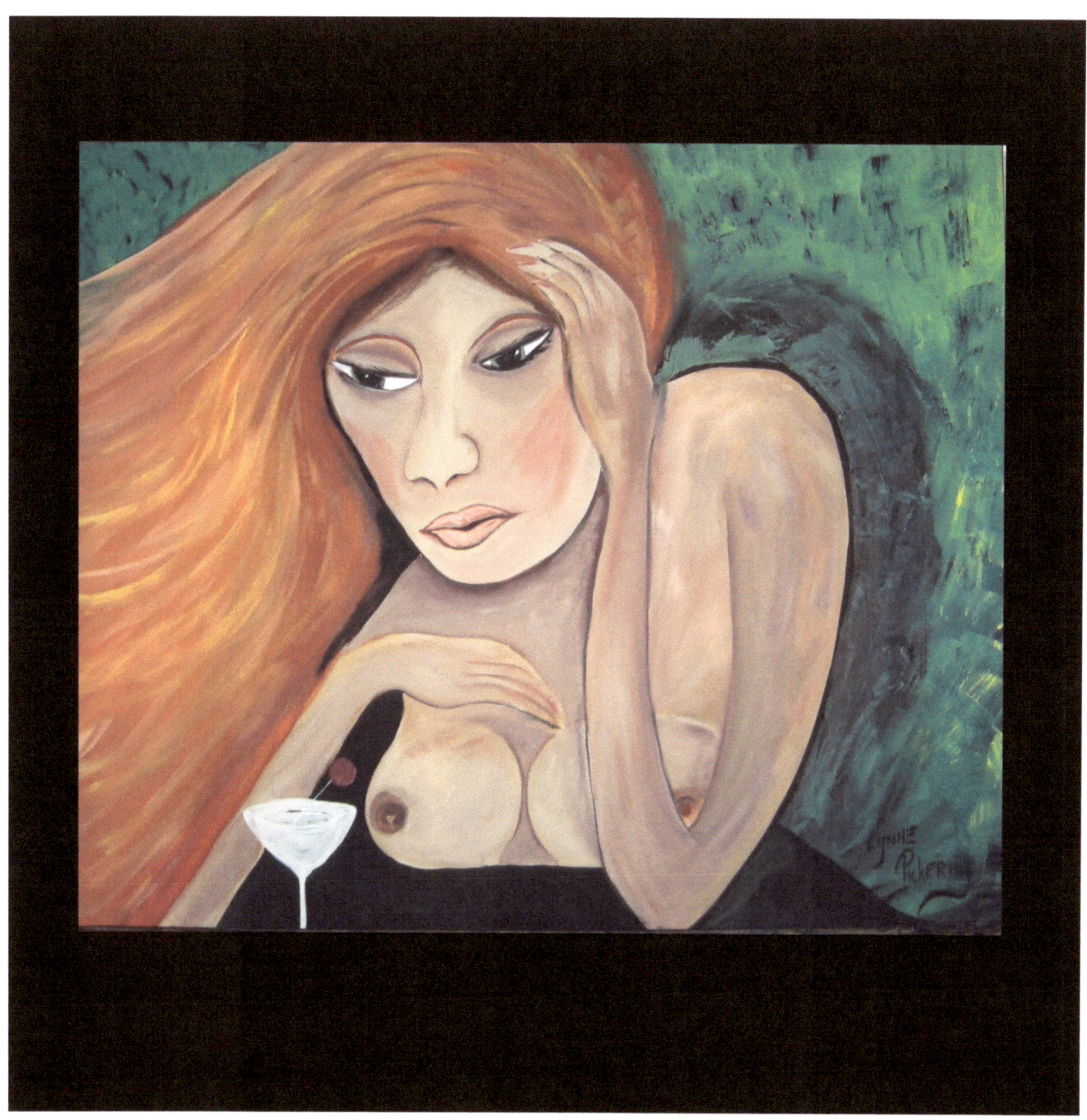

Nude crying 4ft x3ft acrylic

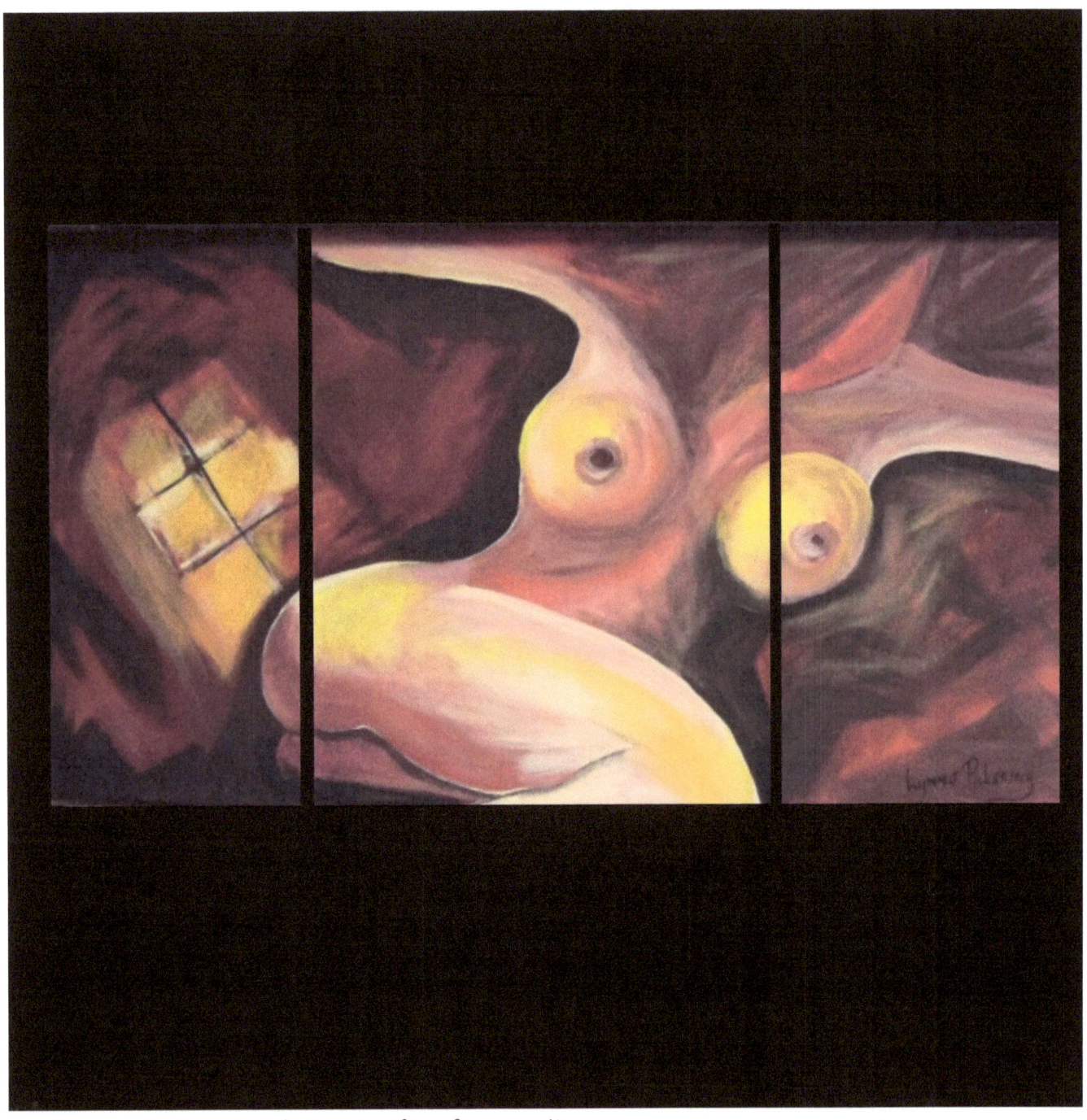

Nude at window in abstract 4ftx2ft acrylic

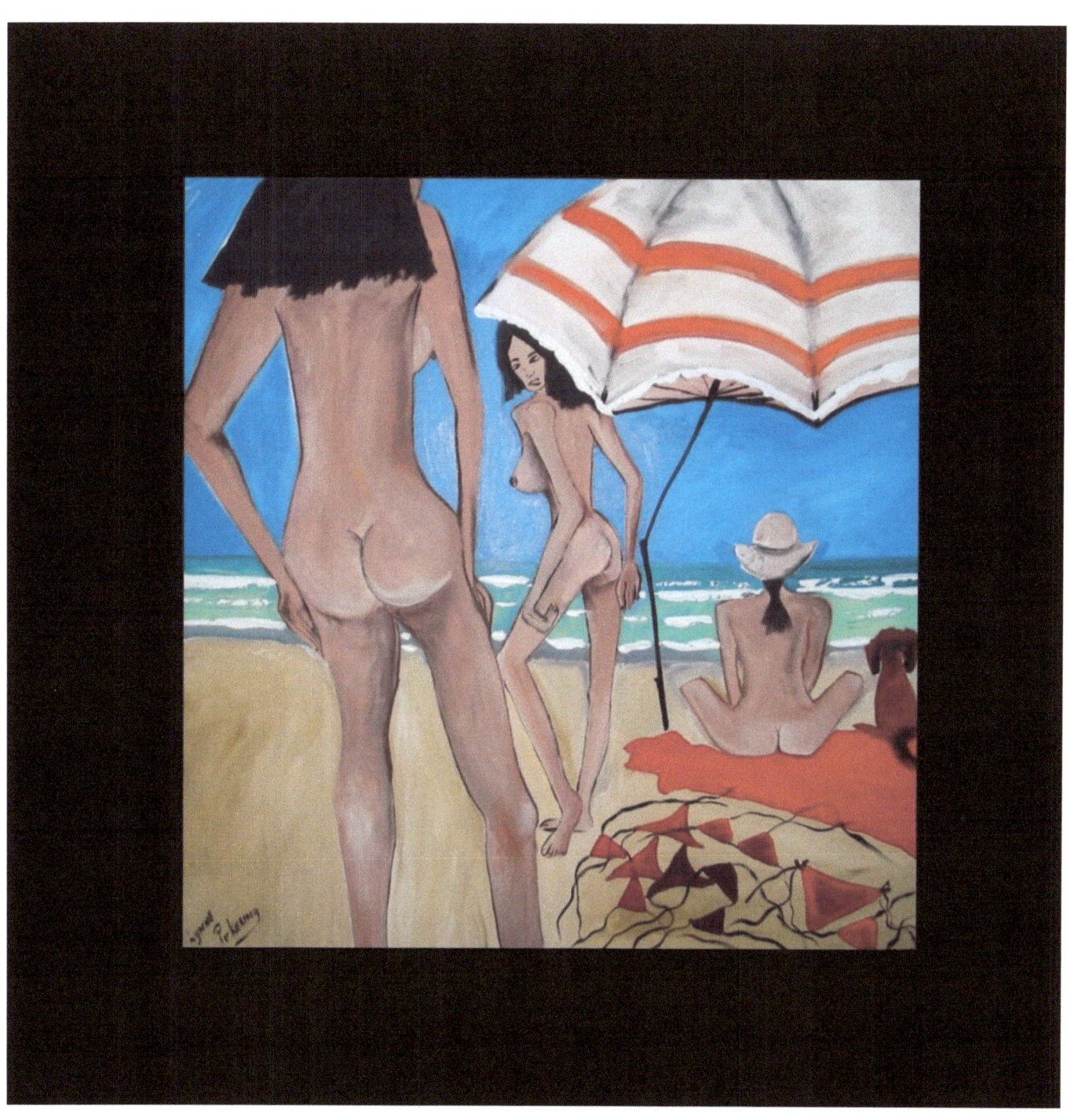

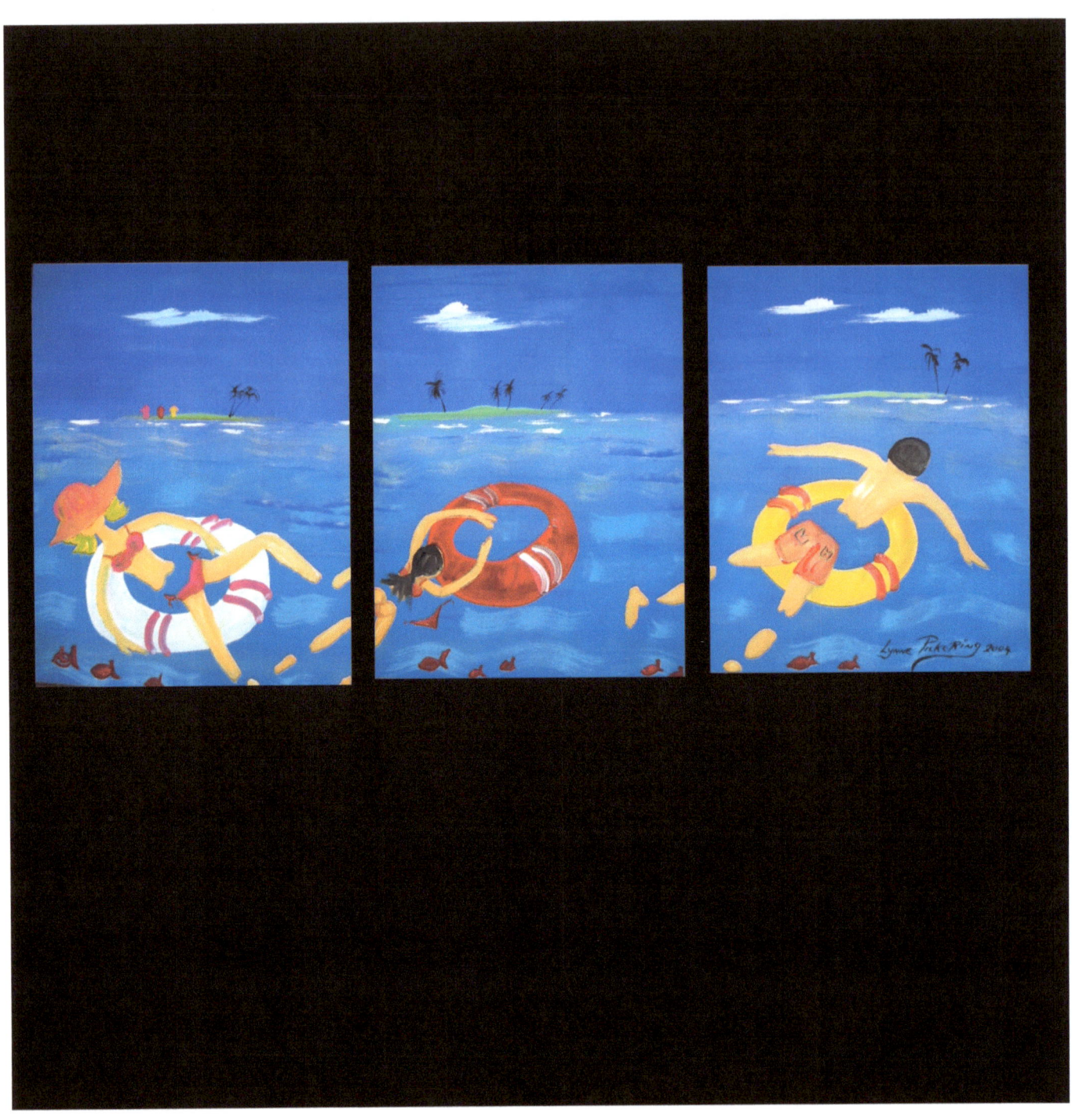

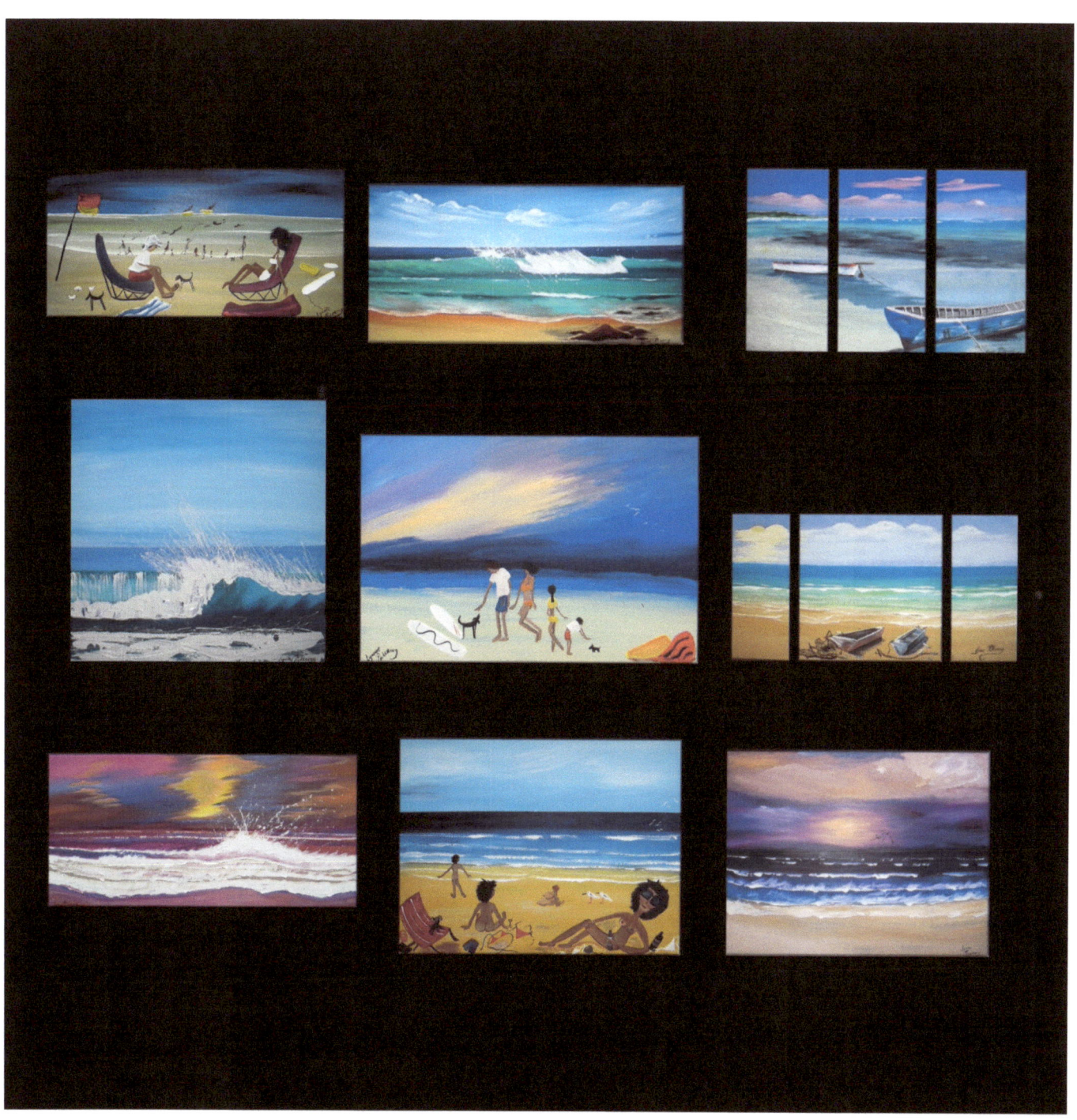

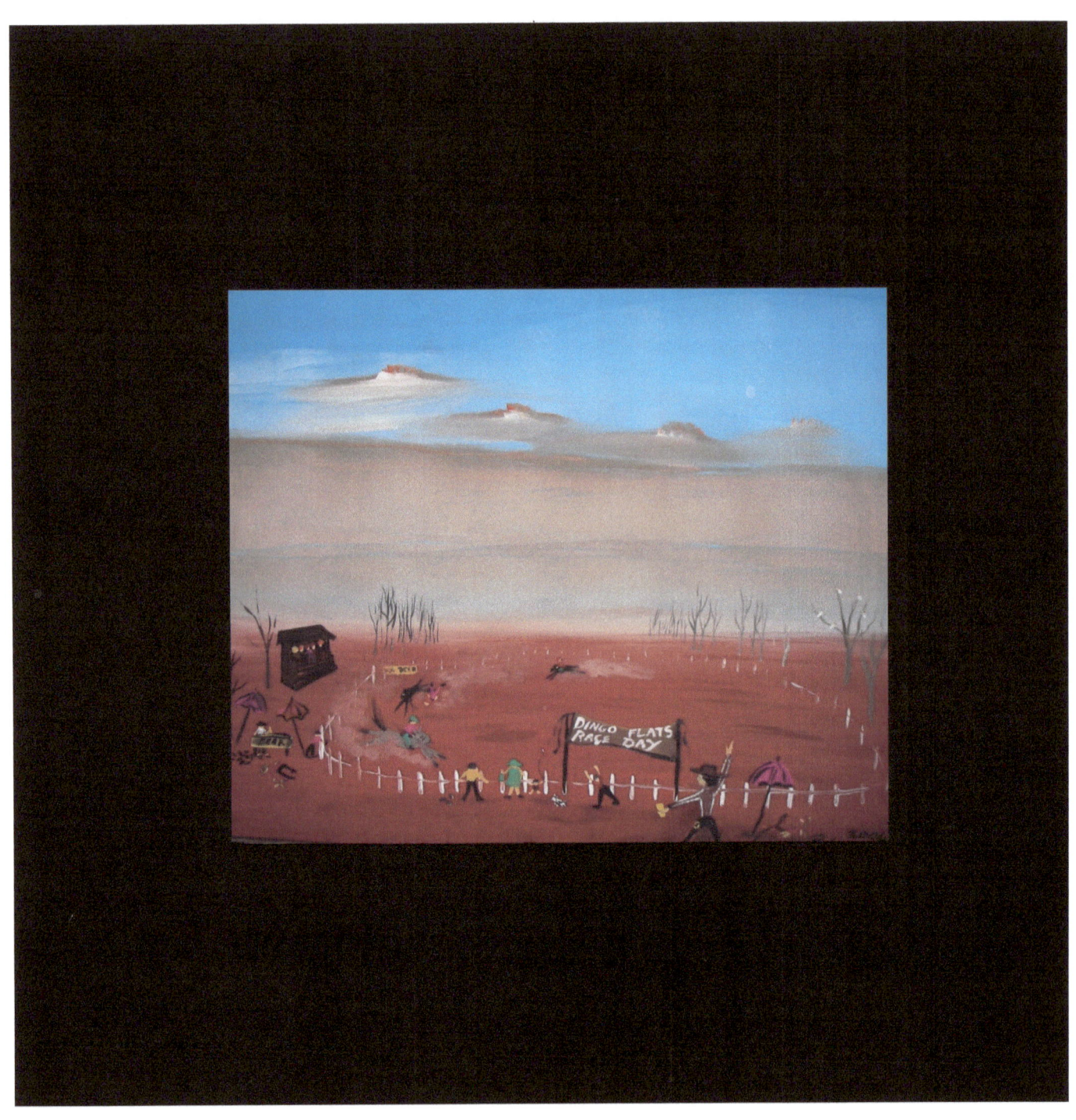

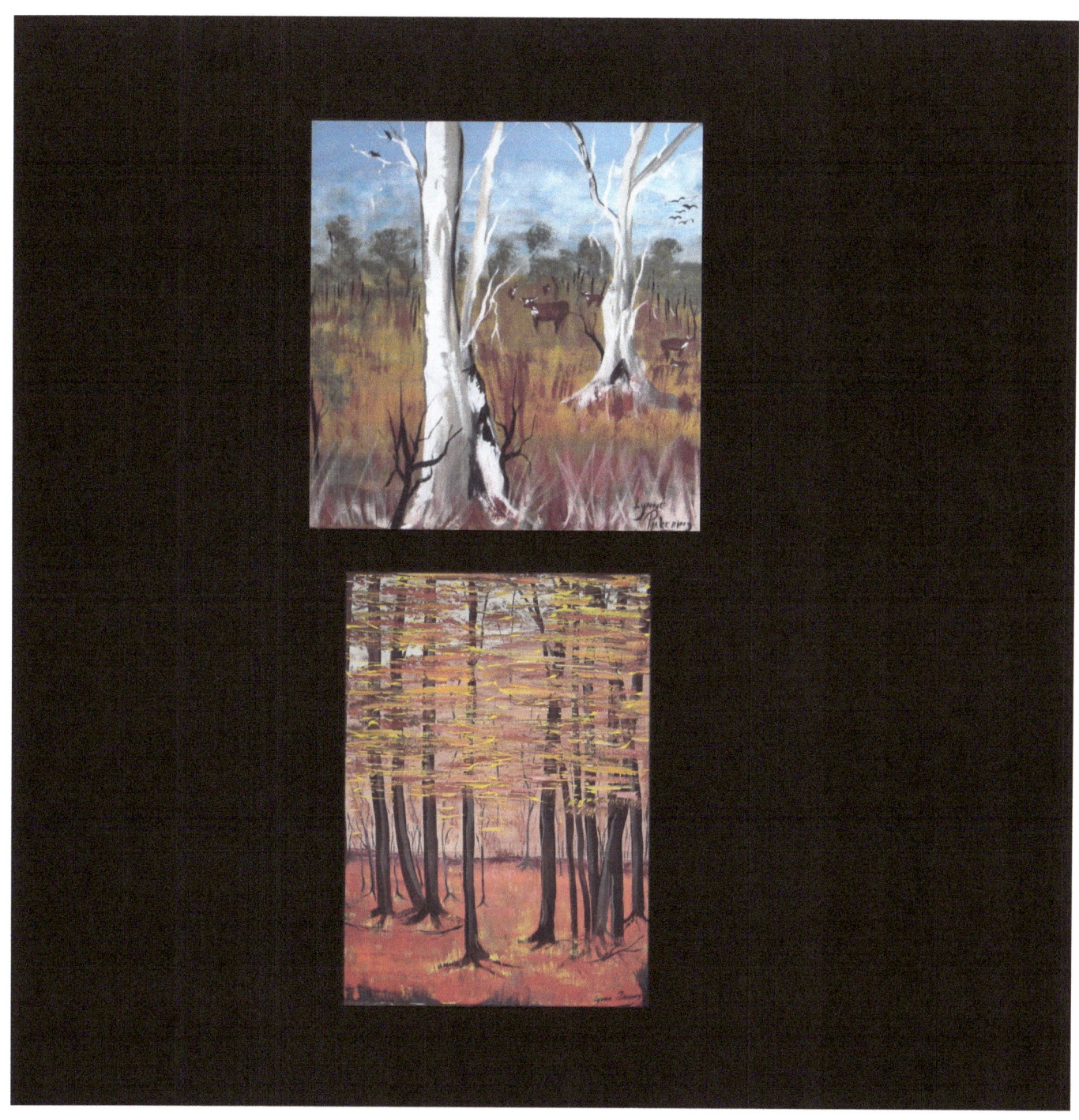

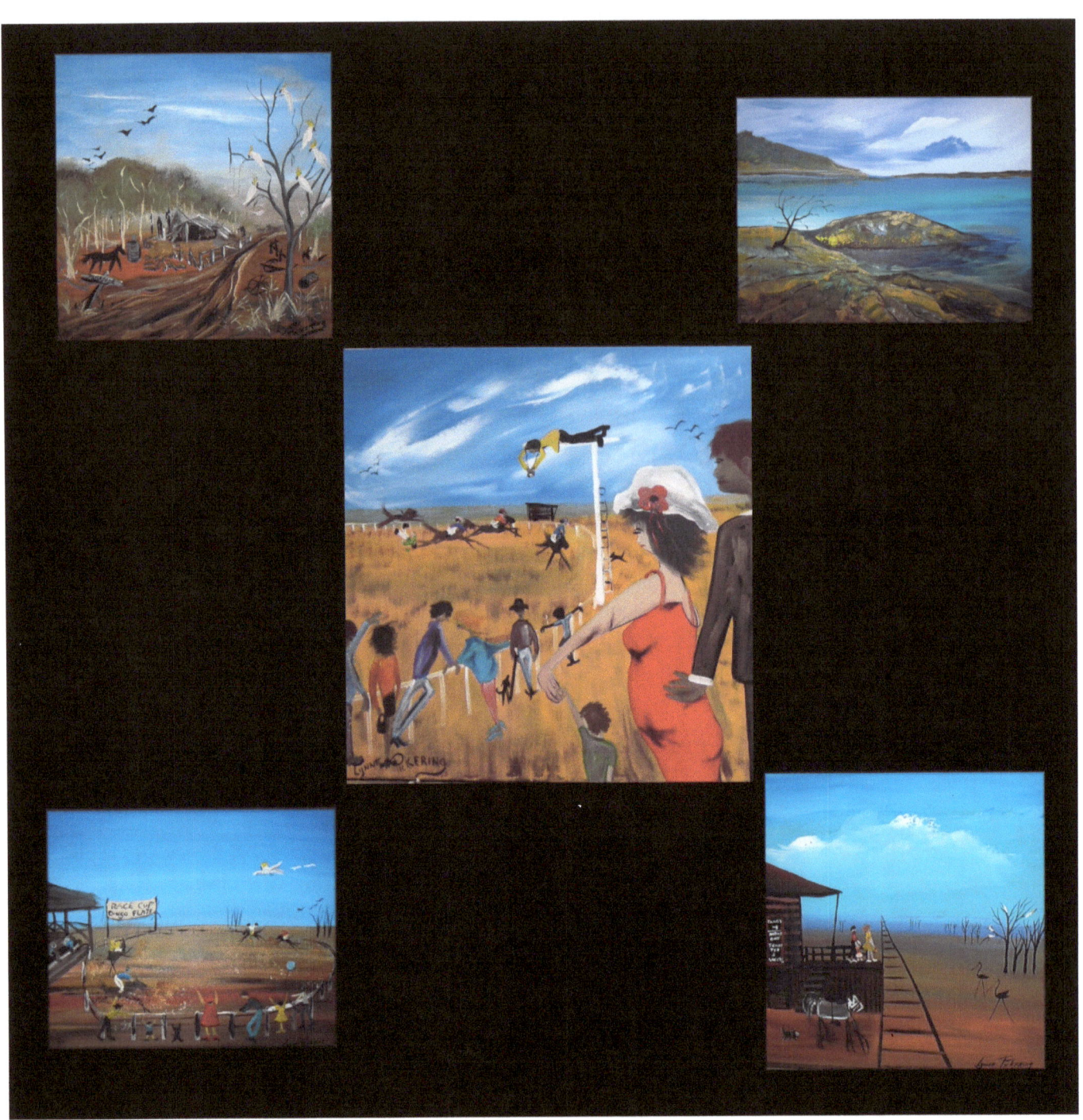

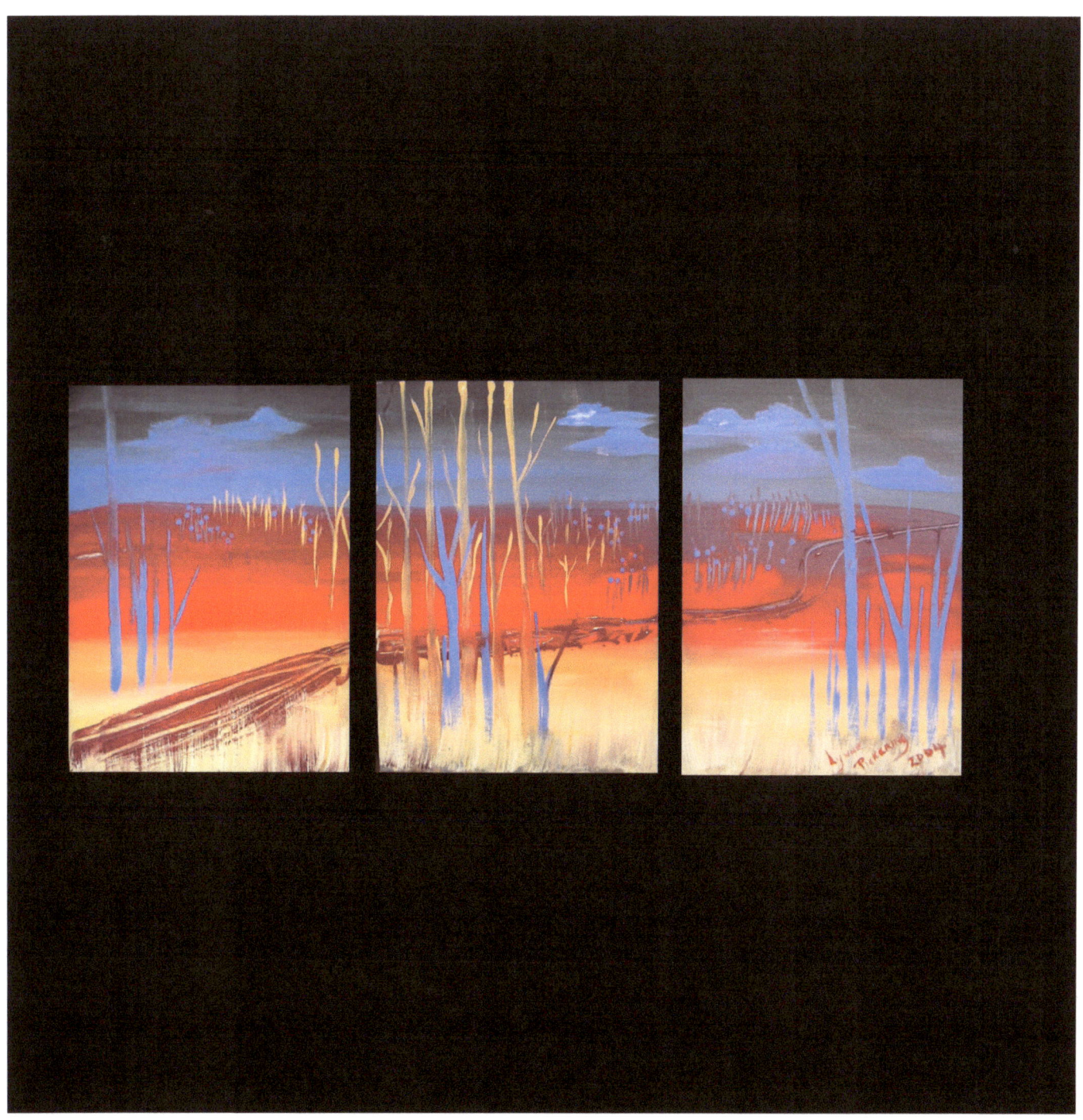

Abstract wall mural 6ft x3ft acrylic

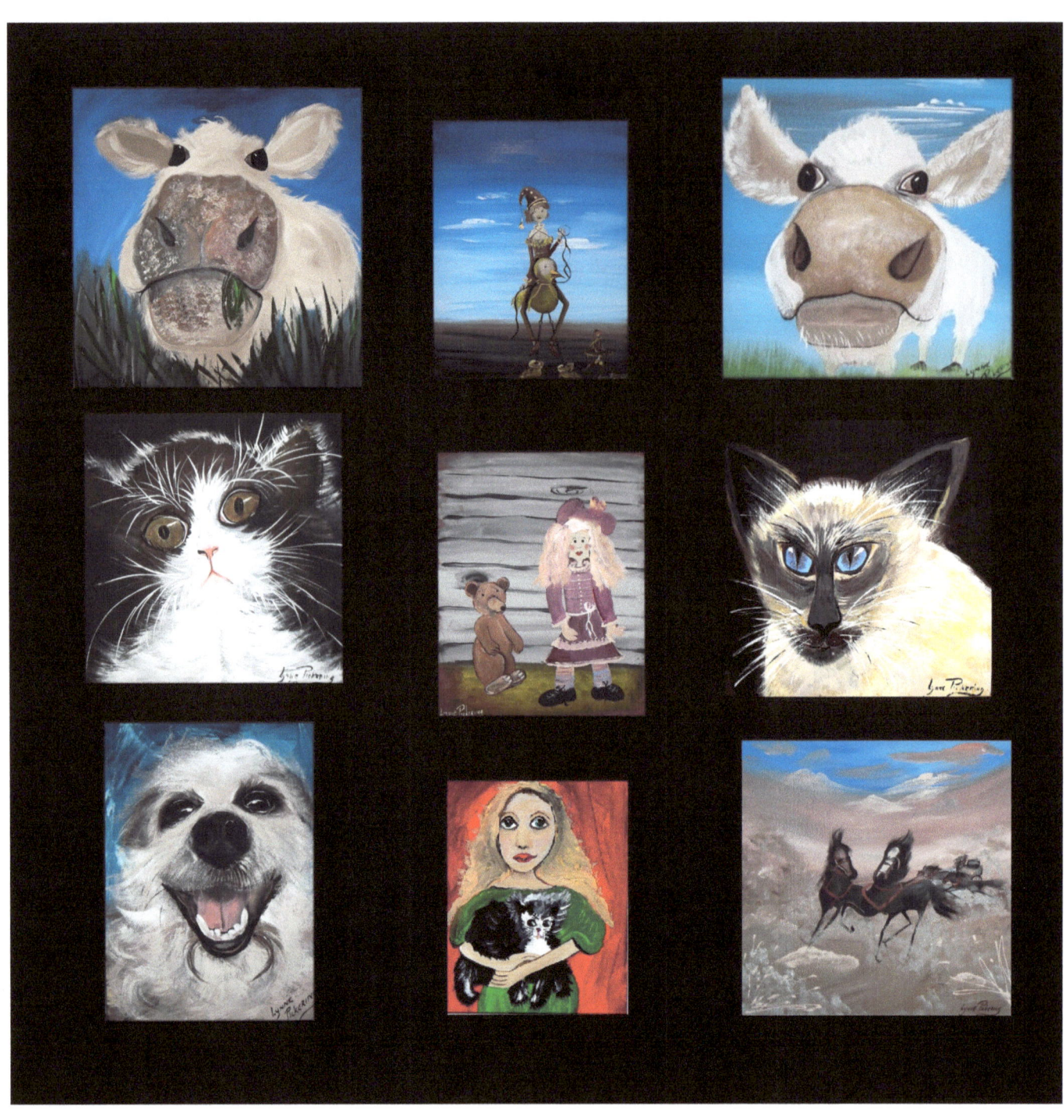

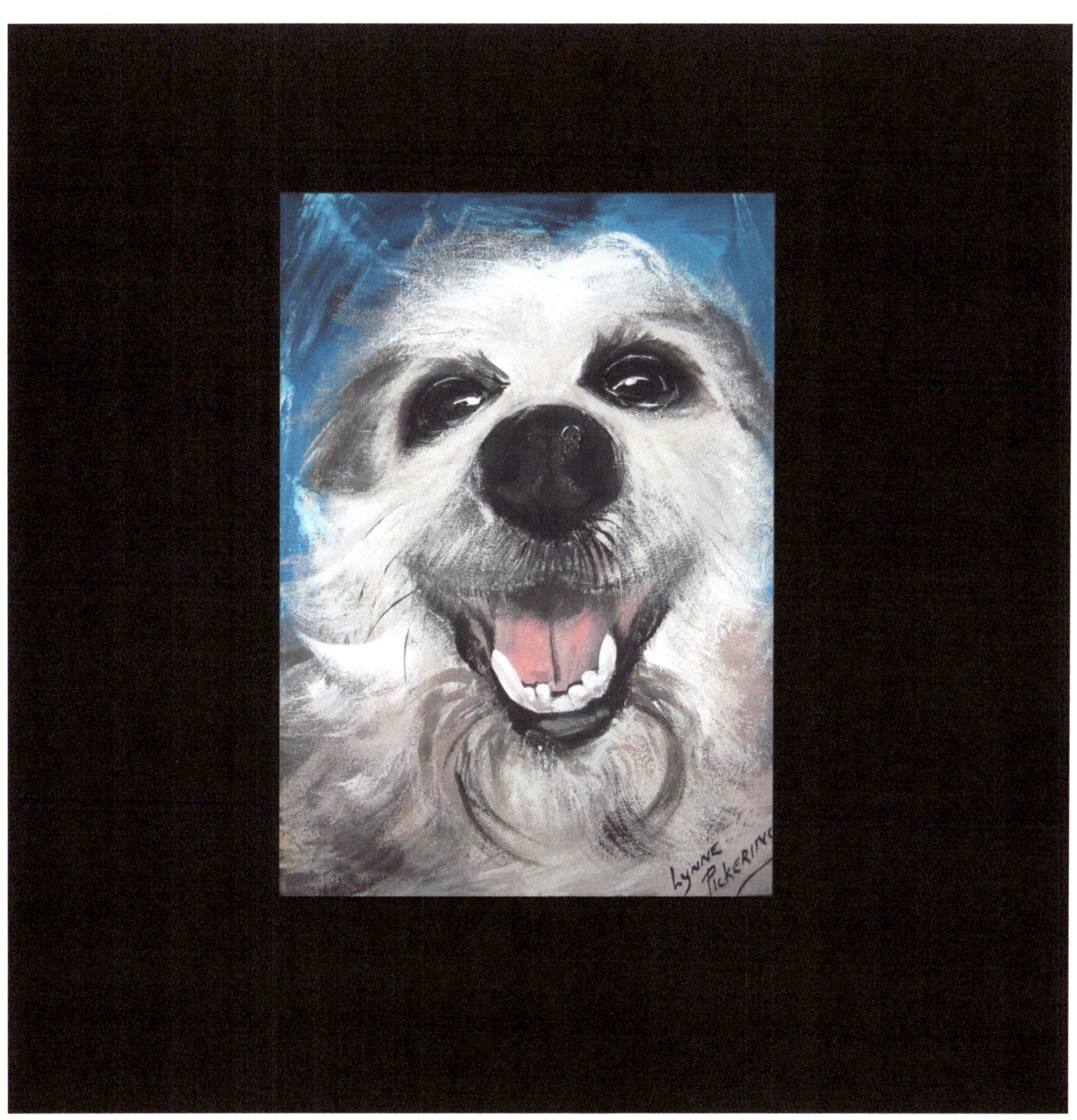

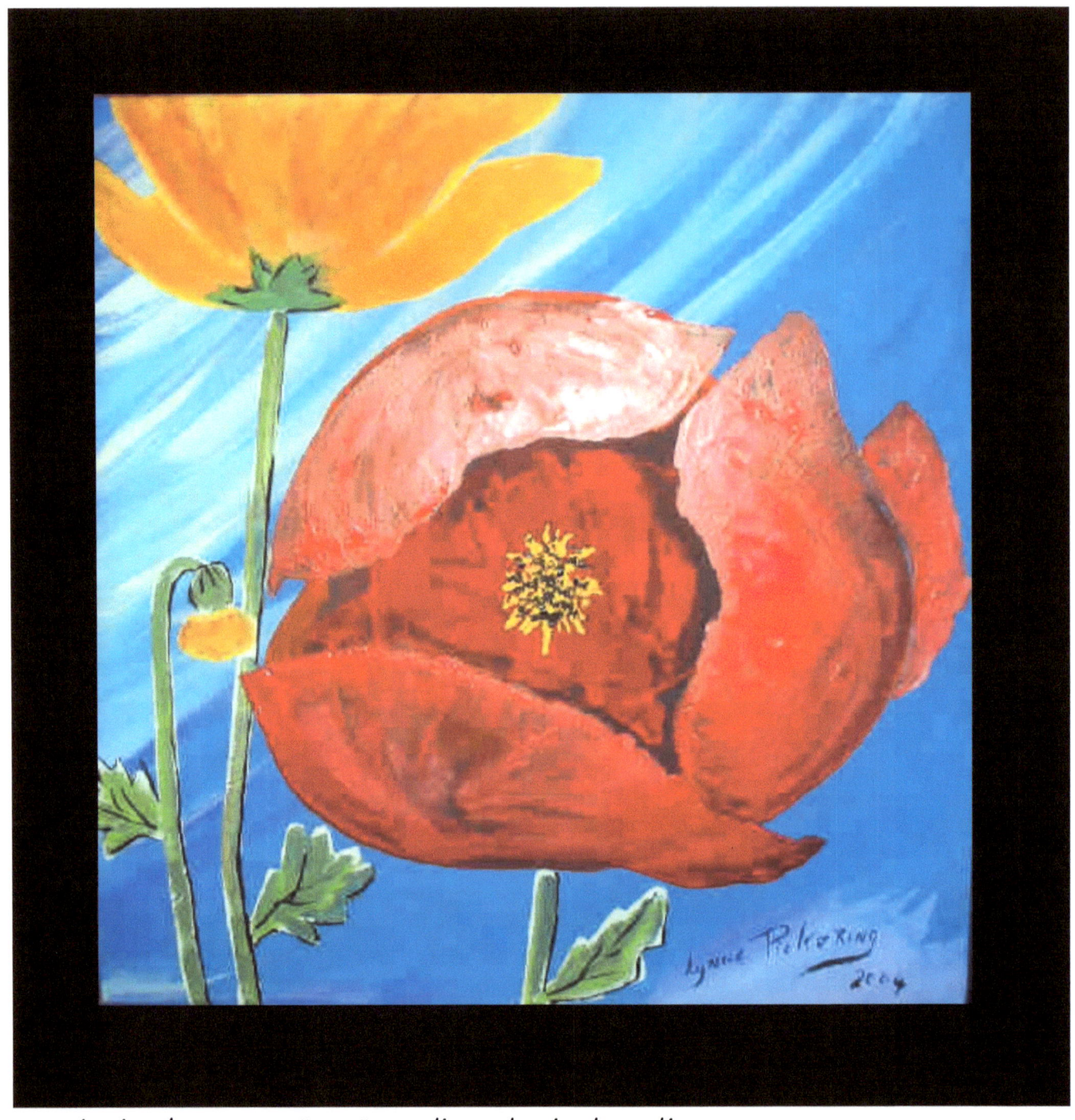

Poppies in abstract 36"x36" acrylic and mixed media

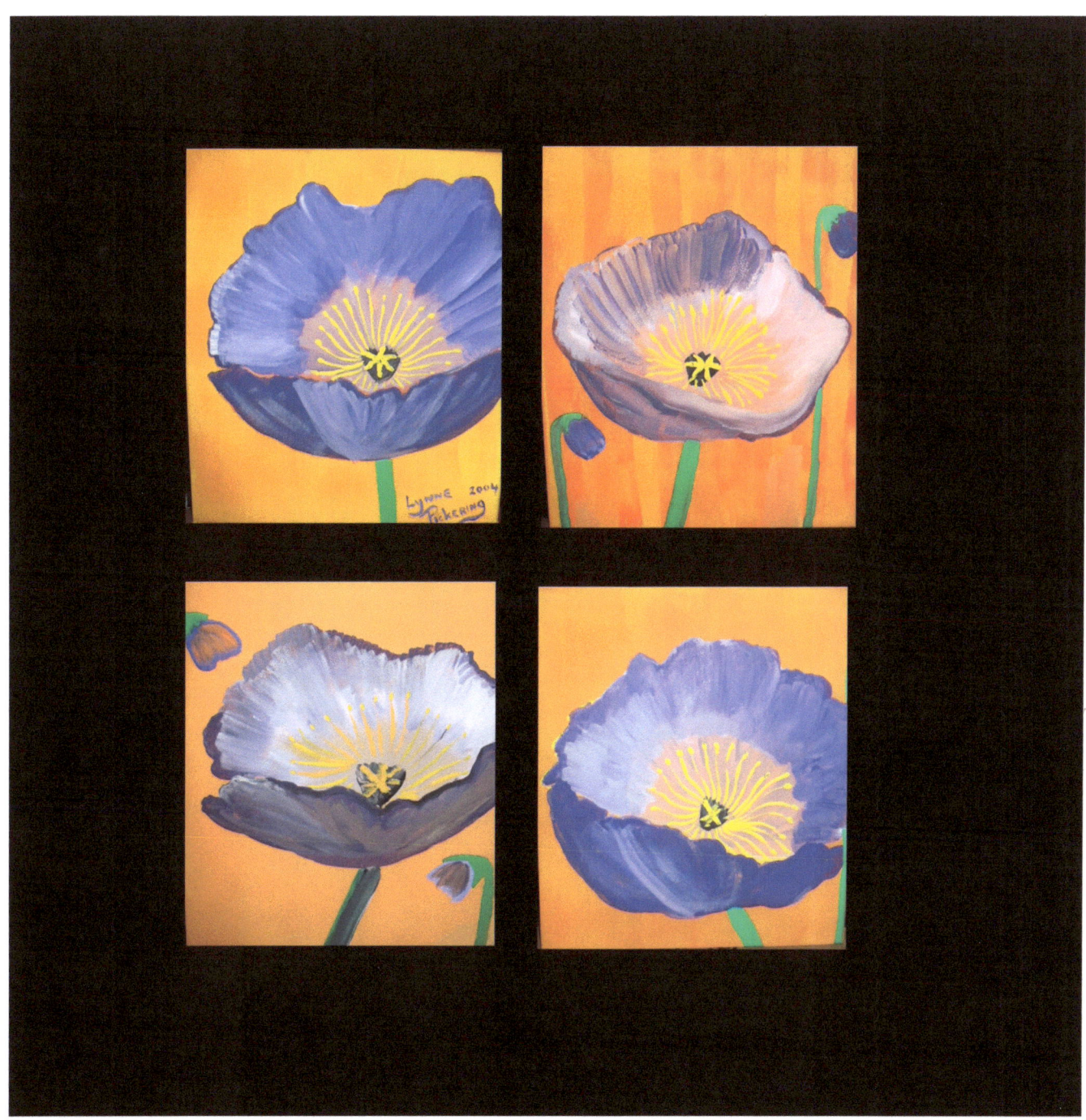

Purple poppies 4ft x6ft wall mural

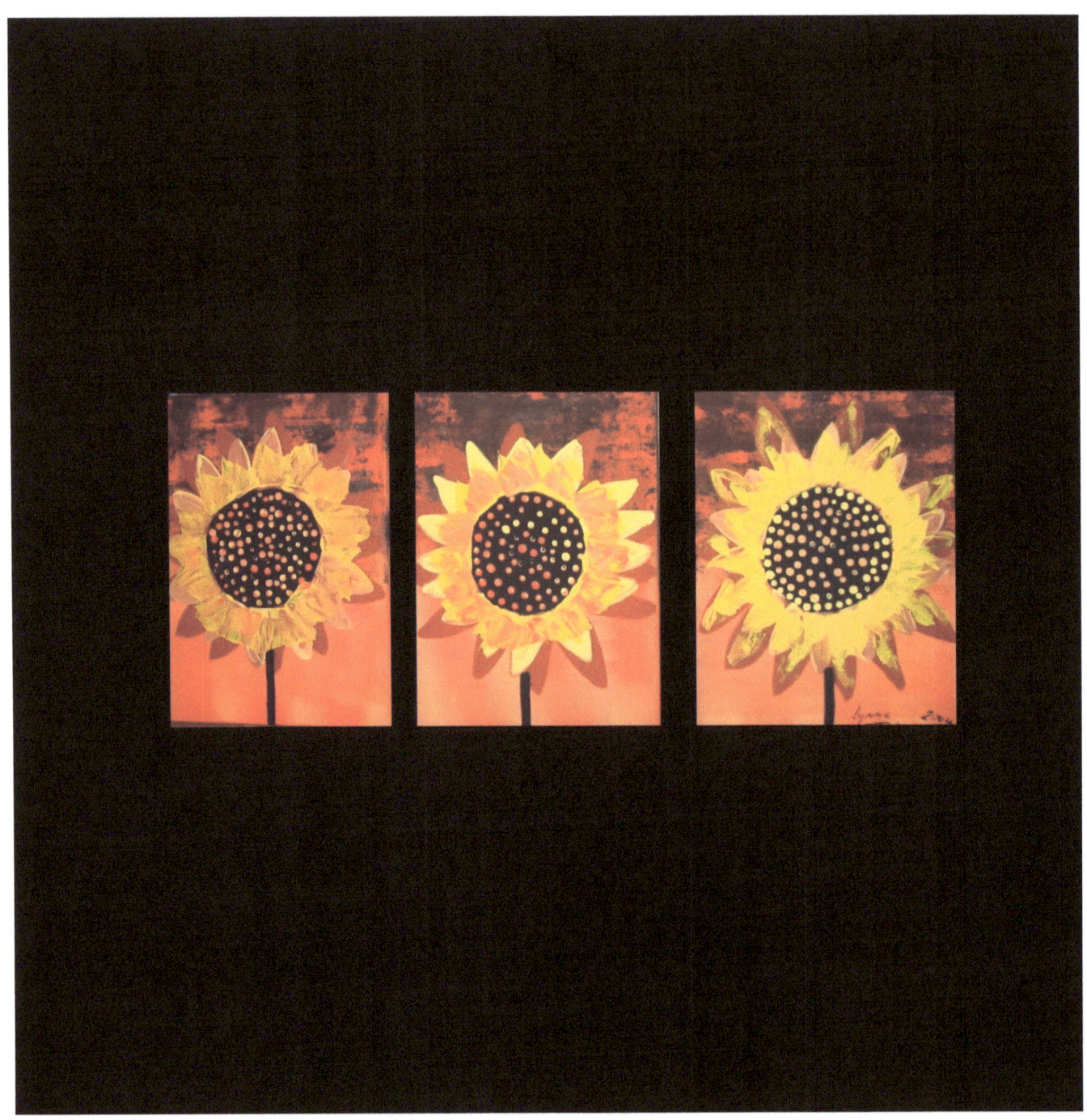

Sunflowers wall mural 6ftx 2ft acrylic

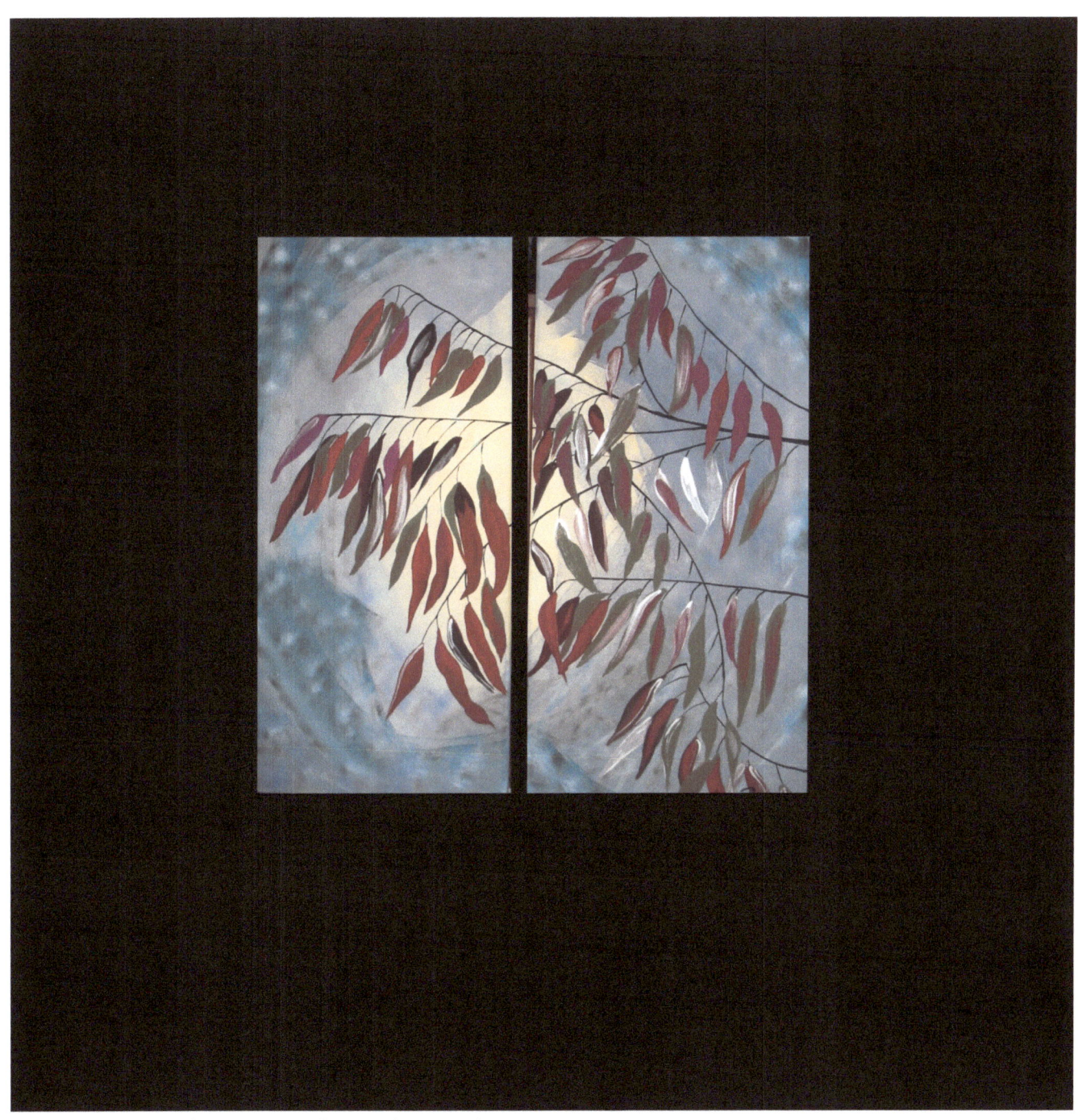

Gum leaves abstract 4ft x 4ft acrylic

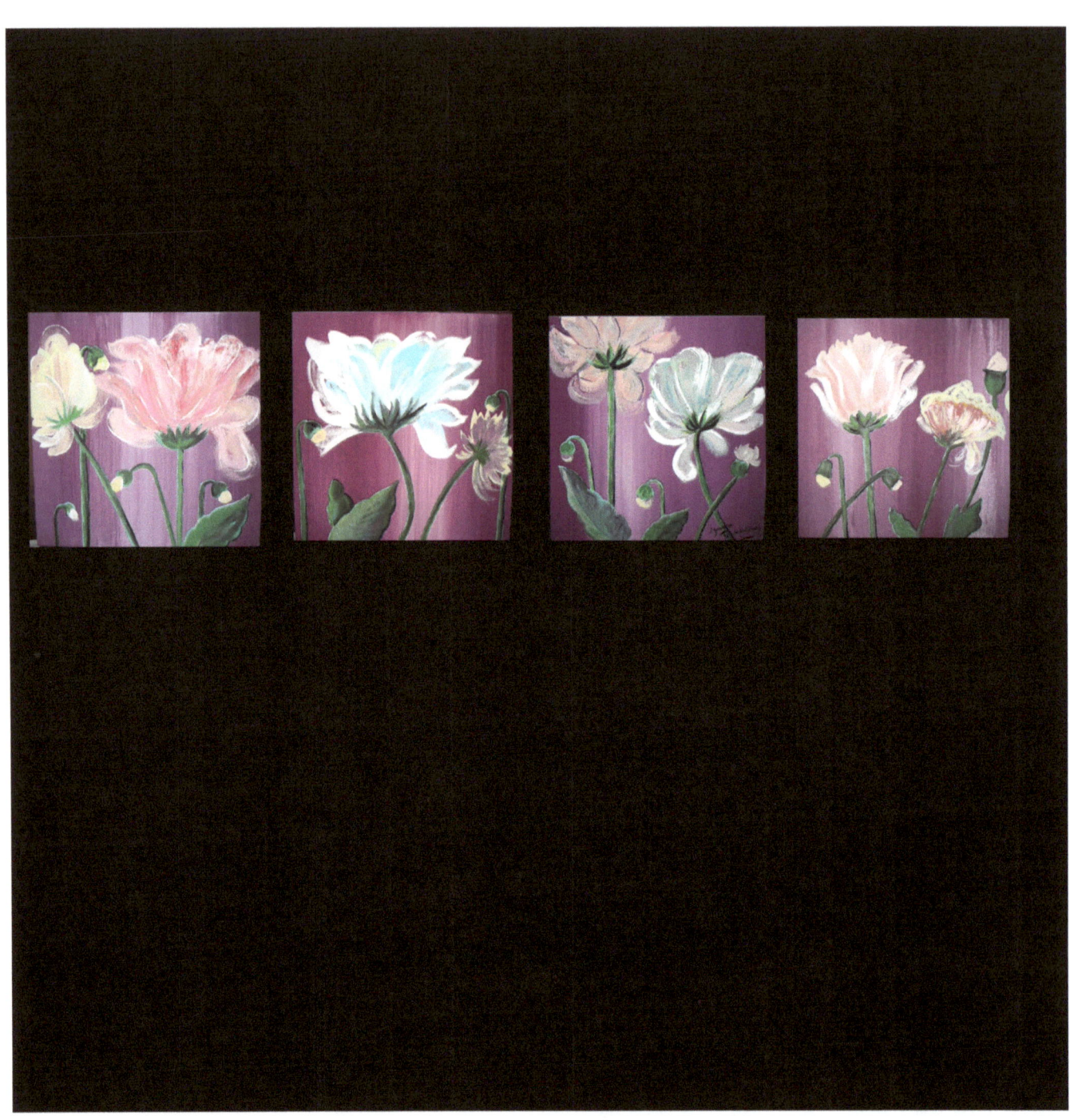

COMMISSIONS :

EMAIL ME ON carealot303@hotmail.com

Corporate, wall murals, home decorating.